Catholics Are Wrong! Says Who?

An Apologetics Resource for Catholics
Seeking Clarity and Confidence

Copyright © 2026

CatholicsAreWrong.com

Published by Kanan Road Publishing

ISBN (paperback): 979-8-9948635-0-3

Cover and Layout by Michael De Hoyos, Jr.

KANAN ROAD
PUBLISHING

CATHOLICS ARE WRONG

An Apologetics Resource for Catholics
Seeking Clarity and Confidence

WILLIAM MORAN

Table of Contents

WHY I WROTE THIS BOOK

What began as a simple invitation to reflect on my spiritual life during a business seminar evolved into a lifelong passion to help others. I did not write this book as a scholar looking down from a distance. I wrote it as a man who wandered, wrestled, and was led home. Although I was raised in a devout Catholic family, I pursued hedonic worldly pleasures. As I became increasingly worldly, I continually felt that something was still missing. There was a constant, low-grade ache for more, although I had no idea what I was aching for.

The invitation came from a born-again Christian who encouraged a relationship with Jesus. It was the "more" that I was looking for. Remembering my Catholic upbringing, I began attending Mass again. I also discovered Christian television preachers who spoke to me in an emotionally resonant way.

At the time, I was unaware of the many different Christian denominations. It was all about Jesus, and it began to fill a void that the world couldn't fill.

As I listened more, I began to hear the anti-Catholic assertions, which left me confused about the truth. Are these preachers who were igniting my emotions right? Were my parents—who were both devout Catholics—wrong?

Although I continued going to Mass, I became increasingly unsettled. Was the Catholic church the *Whore of Babylon*, as some of these preachers claimed? Was the church wrong to have statues, refer to a priest as "father," and pray to Mary? These and many other anti-Catholic accusations left me yearning for answers. One day after leaving Mass, I spotted a flyer in the back of the Church that would lead me on this now thirty-plus-year journey. It was an advertisement for a presentation by Catholic apologist Tim Staples. "Apologist" is a fancy word for defender. It originates from the Greek word *apologia*, meaning "a speech in defense" or "a reasoned argument." Anyone can defend something; an apologist defends it thoughtfully, using logic, evidence, and reason.

Tim's presentation exposed the many (often silly) misrepresentations and sometimes blatant lies of Protestantism. I read Tim's books, listened to his tapes, opened the Scriptures, and began to study the early Church Fathers, councils, and the history of the Church's worship. It was not long before I realized that the Catholic Church had to be the one, true, holy, and apostolic Church referred to in the Nicene Creed, which I recited each Sunday at Mass.

Moreover, the Catholic faith is not an obstacle to a personal relationship with Jesus (many of the Church's detractors believe that such a personal relationship is necessary for salvation). It should be stated that the Catholic faith is where that relationship is nourished, forgiven, and fed.

Since that life-changing invitation during a business seminar, I have made it my side mission to help others discover the same opportunity—the one that leads to a personal relationship with Jesus Christ. This relationship is nurtured through *His Church, as He promised*, and is sustained and deepened by grace, which flows through the sacraments entrusted to His Church. There is nothing more personal than receiving Jesus's Body and Blood in the Eucharist. Through the proclamation of Scripture, the mercy of Confession, and sound teaching, the Church equips disciples to know, love, and follow Christ.

This book exists for three reasons. First, to steady Catholics who feel overwhelmed when someone says, *"Catholics are wrong."* Second, to help bring back the fallen-away, who may have been misled by a Protestant assertion that they have no answer for. Third, to engage non-Catholics with confidence, clarity, and charity, avoiding verse duels—and building, on shared ground, the love of Christ.

When I first began studying apologetics, the internet did not exist—good resources were hard to find and often obscure. By grace, I discovered, read, and in some cases met seasoned apologists like Tim Staples, Jimmy Akin, Rosalind Moss (now Mother Miriam of the Lamb of God), Scott Hahn, Karl Keating, Marcellino D'Ambrosio, Jesse Romero, Peter Kreeft, and others who taught me to love truth with both clarity and charity. Today, of course, there is a flood of material on YouTube and across the web. That abundance is a gift—but it also means we need discernment: not every confident voice is a reliable guide.

My aim in writing this book is simple and, I hope, humble: to demonstrate that even the most sophisticated debates ultimately return to two fundamental realities. First, faith in Christ, who promised to build His Church and to send the Holy Spirit to guide her. Second, the ever-present temptation of pride—the belief that I know better than the Church Christ founded.

That was the root of the first sin in Eden, and it still whispers today. Confidence in the truth and humility before God belong together. When they do, apologetics becomes less about "winning" and more about helping souls find their way home.

If you remember nothing else, remember this: the same Christ who gave us Scripture also gave us the Church that recognizes, safeguards, and interprets it. I hope that these pages provide you with confidence to stand in what you have received, to love what God loves, and to invite others into the fullness of Christ's life in His Church.

Introduction: Why the Question Matters

All Christians should be prepared to give a defense of their hope—"always be ready to make a defense to anyone who asks you for a reason for the hope that is in you; yet do it with gentleness and reverence" (1 Pt 3:15). That means knowing what the Church teaches, why she teaches it, and how to share it with clarity, charity, and calm.

Offering reasons is also an act of love. People deserve thoughtful answers, not slogans. When you explain the hope within you, you treat the other person with dignity and invite real understanding rather than a shouting match. In the process, your own faith grows stronger: speaking it aloud deepens conviction and exposes weak spots that you can shore up (Jas 1:3).

Clear reasons protect against confusion. They keep us from being "tossed to and fro by every wind of doctrine" (Eph 4:14). God often uses reasoned witness to open hearts to grace—think of Paul at the Areopagus (Acts 17) and his counsel to teach with patient clarity (2 Tm 2:24–25).

Finally, good explanations build unity. Jesus Himself prayed for our unity—"that they may all be one ... so that the world may believe" (Jn 17:21). Calm, reasoned dialogue lowers defensiveness and keeps the focus where it belongs—on Christ, on the authority He gave His Church, and on the continuity of the apostolic faith—instead of devolving into "verse tennis."

However, for many Catholics, being told "Catholics are wrong" feels like a punch to the gut. A co-worker quotes a verse, a friend questions the Church's authority, or an online video insists that "the Bible alone" settles everything. In moments like these, faithful people often fall silent—not because they lack faith, but because they are unsure what to say. When the accusations come from someone quoting the Bible chapter and verse, many Catholics often feel intimidated and guilty that they do not know the Bible as well as they should.

Here is the good news: Jesus calls us to childlike humility, trust, and receptivity—while remaining mature in discernment. He does not ask us to be biblical scholars, professional historians, or trained theologians. To respond with confidence, you need only to stand on Christ's own promise. Jesus said to Peter: "You are Peter, and on this rock, I will build my Church, and the gates of hell shall not prevail against it" (Mt 16:18). He also promised to be with His Church "even to the end of the age" (Mt 28:20) and to send the Spirit of Truth to guide the Apostles "into all the truth" (Jn 16:13).

The Catholic claim is simple. It takes Christ at His word. Christ founded a visible Church that would never fail and would lead us into all truth. Furthermore, by His very nature, he cannot lie. With childlike faith (not childish faith), we can trust Him and only Him. It can no doubt feel intimidating when someone fires off chapter and verse that seems to contradict a belief or practice you hold. While you might not have every citation memorized, if you attend Sunday Mass for three years (the A–B–C lectionary cycle) or daily Mass for two years (the weekday cycle), you will hear the vast majority of Scripture proclaimed and likely know the Bible better than you think.

Each Sunday includes an Old Testament reading, a Psalm, a New Testament reading, and a Gospel. So, the next time someone claims Catholics do not read the Bible, remember: the Church proclaims it—publicly, systematically, and constantly. Additionally, every Sunday, Catholics proclaim the Nicene

Creed. Many people take the creed for granted, unaware of its origins. This profession of faith arose early to defend the heart of the Gospel. The creed is a key that also demonstrates that, from its beginning, the Church was functioning as Christ intended: gathering bishops, clarifying doctrine, safeguarding unity for the whole world, and leading its followers "into all truth."

After setting the stage with a brief background about the church, I will share a simple three-step method for responding to the claim "Catholics are wrong." Nobody likes to hear "you are wrong." Our natural inclination is to feel defensive. You do not need to be on the defensive; you have *the truth* on your side. The goal is not to win an argument or be right; the goal is to help find the truth. Establishing terms and common ground, and asking questions, compels a good-faith interlocutor to reevaluate their position and seek the truth independently.

This book is not a survey of every denomination—that would take several volumes. There are thousands of Protestant communities; while many overlap, they also differ on matters of doctrine, worship, and authority. For clarity, I will use "Protestant" as a broad label for groups that profess faith in Jesus Christ but are not in communion with Rome.

The Catholic claim—and the organizing logic of this book—is the same across those differences: Christ founded one visible Church with apostolic succession; communities that arose later were founded by individual men, not instituted by Christ, and (as the Catholic Church understands it) do not retain the sacramental succession handed on by the Apostles.

A few movements teach that historic Christianity apostatized and had to be "restored"—for example, Joseph Smith (Latter-day Saints), Charles Taze Russell (Jehovah's Witnesses), and Felix Manalo (Iglesia ni Cristo).

In the end, most Protestants affirm the Apostles' teaching, yet their narrative often implies a functional restoration: the Church supposedly drifted so far into error that it had to be recovered in the sixteenth century. They may not use the word *apostasy* as, say, Mormons do, but the claim is similar in effect—Christ's Church became corrupt and failed, necessitating a restoration.

That stance collides with Jesus's promise that "the gates of hell shall not prevail" against His Church (Mt 16:18). The choice is stark: either Christ keeps His public promise to preserve His visible Church in the truth, or His Church failed and required restoration. Both cannot be true.

A brief word on the Orthodox Churches: the formal break with Rome is usually dated to 1054 CE (though earlier tensions existed). The Eastern Orthodox share the Catholic Church's core dogmas (Trinity, full divinity and humanity of Christ, seven sacraments, apostolic succession, real Eucharistic presence, veneration of saints, ancient Creeds).

The separation (the "Great Schism," conventionally dated to 1054) is primarily about ecclesial communion and papal primacy/jurisdiction, not a rejection of the central dogmas of the faith. Our disagreements are serious, yet they are of a different kind than those with post-Reformation communities. Rome describes the Orthodox as true Churches with valid sacraments and apostolic succession but not in full communion with the Bishop of Rome.

Many observers—Catholic and Orthodox—believe that real reconciliation is possible because so much of what divides us is *how* we speak, not *what* we believe. East and West already share the apostolic essentials: valid bishops and sacraments, the Eucharistic Real Presence, baptismal regeneration, veneration of Mary and the saints, and the same ancient Creeds. The main disagreements—papal authority, how the Creed describes the Holy Spirit, and certain church customs—are usually about how things are expressed and practiced, not about denying core Christian beliefs. The East acknowledges a special leadership role tied to Peter but questions how that leadership should be exercised; differences in Creed language are often about wording rather than substance; and practical matters like fasting and calendars can vary without changing the heart of the faith.

Recent dialogues have repeatedly shown that we sometimes talk past one another. The path forward is a primacy lived in a way that the East can receive and a synodality that the West can recognize—so that the one apostolic faith we already share can be fully lived in visible communion, answering the Lord's prayer "that they all may be one" (Jn 17:21).

CHAPTER 1

THE CREED AND THE CHURCH

Many Catholics will recognize the Nicene Creed, since it is recited at every Sunday Mass. What they may not know is the creed's origins. Understanding the origins, however, is a key to bridging the divide and answering the charge that "Catholics are wrong." Ironically, many Protestants also accept this same creed, even if they do not recite it; they accept its professions. Lutheran, Anglican, many Reformed/Presbyterians, and Methodists may recite it. While some evangelical/free-church groups do not use formal creeds, they would still affirm their content regarding the Trinity and the Incarnation.

The Nicene Creed

> *I believe in one God, the Father almighty, maker of heaven and earth, of all things visible and invisible.*
>
> *I believe in one Lord Jesus Christ, the Only*

Begotten Son of God, born of the Father before all ages.

God from God, Light from Light, true God from true God, begotten, not made, consubstantial with the Father; through him all things were made. For us men and for our salvation, he came down from heaven, and by the Holy Spirit was incarnate of the Virgin Mary and became man.

For our sake, he was crucified under Pontius Pilate, he suffered death and was buried, and rose again on the third day in accordance with the Scriptures.

He ascended into heaven and is seated at the right hand of the Father.

He will come again in glory to judge the living and the dead, and his kingdom will have no end.

I believe in the Holy Spirit, the Lord, the giver of life, who proceeds from the Father and the Son, who with the Father and the Son is adored and glorified, who has spoken through the prophets.

I believe in one, holy, catholic, and apostolic Church.

I confess one baptism for the forgiveness of sins, and I look forward to the resurrection of the dead and the life of the world to come. Amen.

For most Christians, the doctrine of the Trinity is an assumption; however, the Bible does not use the word "Trinity," and the doctrine is not explicitly spelled out in a single verse. The Nicene Creed (325/381 CE) gathers the biblical data—Father, Son, and Holy Spirit—into a clear confession: one God in three Persons.

Because this expresses what Scripture teaches in sum, most Protestants rightly recognize and profess the Creed, even while holding to "Scripture alone." In practice, they are accepting a Spirit-guided, Church-defined summary of biblical truth—an example of apostolic Tradition serving Scripture, not competing with it.

At this point, you might wonder why a Protestant would accept the creed when it says explicitly, "I believe in one, holy, *Catholic* and apostolic Church." The Reformers believed they were reforming the Church, not founding a new one, so they retained the ancient, ecumenical creeds—especially those concerning the Trinity and Christ's divinity—while disputing later claims about authority, sacraments, and other matters.

Therefore, they explicitly say Catholic does not mean "Roman Catholic" but "the whole body of Christ across times and places." We will see later how this is true, but not in the way a Protestant might think.

Why the Creed? Background and Purpose

In 325 CE, the First Council of Nicaea addressed the Arian crisis—Arius claimed that the Son was a creature and not fully God. Arius was a Christian presbyter from Alexandria, Egypt, whose teaching sparked the fourth-century Arian controversy. He argued that the Son (the Word) is not co-eternal with the Father but a created being—exalted above all creatures, yet still "there was when he was not." This made the Son subordinate to the Father in being (not just role), denying the full divinity of Christ. Arius spread his views in sermons, songs (his lost work Thalia), and letters, winning support among some clergy and imperial officials. Emperor Constantine convened the council, and roughly three hundred bishops gathered from across the Christian world. Notable churchmen included Alexander of Alexandria, accompanied by his deacon Athanasius, as well as Eusebius of Caesarea, Eustathius of Antioch, and others. These bishops—successors of the Apostles—safeguarded the apostolic faith, confessed the Son as "consubstantial" (of

one substance) with the Father, and anathema-
tized Arianism. Nicaea's purpose was to defend the
full divinity of Christ and preserve the unity of the
Church's worship and preaching.

Formulated first at Nicaea and later expanded
at Constantinople (381 CE), the Nicene Creed
expressed the Church's visible unity in doctrine and
worship. Note that this creed—written before the
biblical canon was formally fixed—shows the Church
already exercising her teaching office and handing
on the apostolic faith. The pope at the time—Sylvester I (r. 314–35 CE)—didn't attend Nicaea (325) in
person. He sent legates (traditionally named Vitus
and Vincentius) to represent the Roman See. It was
common practice for the bishop of Rome to be
represented rather than travel such a long, difficult journey. Rome's delegates signed the acts, and
Pope Sylvester later ratified the council's decisions
and creed, which the Church at Rome received and
proclaimed.

In other words, the same Church that later recognized which books belong to the Bible was already
functioning in council, led by bishops in apostolic
succession, to define and defend the truth about
Christ. Although many trinitarian Protestants accept
the doctrine because they see it as accurately teaching Scripture, they deny the councils' inherent infallibility. In other words, the council just happened to

get it right, in their opinion. In non-trinitarian circles, Nicaea is outright rejected. The non-trinitarian claims to be reading the same Bible and guided by the same Holy Spirit that the Protestants and Catholic claim. Who is right?

That is the nub of the matter: authority. For any non-Catholic position, the final authority is either the individual, a local/denominational board, or an informal teaching network—none of which can claim public, apostolic mandate for the *whole* Church. The Catholic answer uniquely offers a coherent chain: Christ → apostles → successors by laying on of hands → a living Magisterium that guards Scripture and Tradition. Without such a center, unity becomes voluntary alignment rather than binding communion; with it, the Church can actually be what Scripture calls her: one, holy, catholic, and apostolic.

The Four Marks of the Church

The four marks of the Church (professed in the Nicene Creed) are:

1. **One**—the Church is His Bride (Eph 5:25-27), so His saving work would continue to be visible throughout history—united in one faith, one baptism, one Lord; called to visible and spiritual unity.

2. **Holy**–set apart by God (Eph 5:25–27), made holy by Christ and the Holy Spirit (despite sinners within).

3. **Catholic**–"universal" (Mt 28:19–20): the same Gospel for all peoples, times, and places.

4. **Apostolic**–founded on the Apostles (Eph 2:19–20): faithful to their teaching and continued through apostolic succession in the Church's leadership.

Apostolic Succession Is Historical

The handing-on of ministry from the Apostles to their successors is a matter of history as well as theology. Early Christian authors listed the succession of bishops in key churches to show continuity with the Apostles. The Church at Rome, for example, preserved a known line of bishops from Peter and Paul forward. This chain of ordination and teaching explains how the same faith has been preserved and recognized across generations. The Apostle Paul:

> So, Christ himself gave the apostles, the prophets, the evangelists, the pastors and teachers, to equip his people for works of service, so that the body of Christ may be built up until we all reach unity in the faith and in the knowledge of the Son of God

and become mature, attaining to the whole measure of the fullness of Christ. Then we will no longer be infants, tossed back and forth by the waves, and blown here and there by every wind of teaching and by the cunning and craftiness of people in their deceitful scheming. Instead, speaking the truth in love, we will grow to become in every respect the mature body of him who is the head, that is, Christ. From him the whole body, joined and held together by every supporting ligament, grows and builds itself up in love, as each part does its work. (Eph 4:11–26)

Moreover, Paul, when writing to Timothy: "What you have heard from me before many witnesses entrust to faithful men who will be able to teach others also" (2 Tm 2:2).

Catholicism Is Not a Denomination

Contemporary Christians, and even some Catholics, assume that Catholicism is a denomination. A denomination, however, is a branch from a prior whole. The word Catholic means universal, and the word universal means for all people, all times, and in all places. The Catholic Church is not a branch; it is the original, visible Church Christ founded. While later groups separated from full communion with the Apostolic See, Catholicism remains the root, not an offshoot. Their bishops have an unbroken succession to the Apostles and preserve valid sacraments, liturgy, and doctrine from the early Church.

Before the Reformation: Simply "The Church"

For centuries, the Christian church was simply referred to as "the Church." Only after later separations did labels like "Roman Catholic" emerge to distinguish those remaining in full communion with the original Church from groups that had broken communion. When asked, Martin Luther, who began the Reformation, did not see himself as breaking from the Church; he referred to those who did not follow his reforms as Roman Catholics. The name in public usage shifted; the Church did not.

Today, people often ask, "Are you Christian or are you Catholic?" That is a muddled question—one that even confuses some Catholics, because Catholics are Christians. The Catholic Church is the original, historic Church from which later communities separated.

When someone asks, "Are you Christian or Catholic?" what they usually mean is, "Are you Protestant or Catholic?" Protestants have come to use Christian as shorthand for non-Catholic Christian, which unintentionally turns Catholics into something other than Christian. That's a category mistake.

The real distinction is between Christian-Protestants and Christian-Catholics—two expressions of the same faith, differing in authority, sacraments, and historical continuity.

Heresies and Councils: The Church's Ongoing Defense

From the beginning, there were disagreements about Christian teachings. In the Acts of the Apostles, we see the debate about circumcision. Throughout the centuries, individuals with their own ideas have attempted to introduce false teachings, and the Church has stood against them—clarifying doctrine in councils and safeguarding the faithful in worship and daily life.

The Protestant movement of the sixteenth century, led by Martin Luther, a Catholic monk, rightly criticized the actions of some corrupt bishops. However, he went beyond mere criticism; he had his own ideas about the faith. His new beliefs did not align with the Church's long-held teachings—to the extent that he declared some books that had been included in the Bible for 1,500 years to be apocryphal (of doubtful authenticity). These books were placed in the back of Luther's new Bible and eventually removed altogether. In other words, Martin Luther, all by himself, changed the canon of the Bible. Throughout its history, the Church has held councils, as it did at Nicaea, to reaffirm or clarify the teachings of the faith that come into question. In response to the theological challenges posed by Martin Luther and the Protestant Reformation, the Church convened the Council of Trent, which met from 1545 to 1563.

His movement, commonly referred to as the "reformation," was in fact no reformation at all and a lie. A reformation implies that the church was being restored to its original state. Luther's teachings, however, had never been taught before. There was no apostolic teaching to revert to, only Luther's own ideas, which resulted in a brand-new theology. What Luther actually did was start a revolution.

The Council reaffirmed the canon of Scripture and clarified the doctrine of justification, which, after 1,500 years, a lone monk had decided was incorrect. It also provided a comprehensive articulation of the nature and number of the sacraments. It is worth noting that Martin Luther still affirmed many of the core Christian doctrines shared with Catholics—the Trinity and Christ's full divinity, the Incarnation, *Mary as Mother of God* (including her perpetual virginity), the necessity of grace, baptismal regeneration, and a real presence of Christ in the Lord's

Supper (understood differently from Catholic transubstantiation, but not a mere symbol).

Since the time of Luther, however, Christianity has splintered into thousands more denominations. Each claim to teach the truth about the faith appeals to the Bible as its ultimate authority—yet they often reach conflicting conclusions. Many Christians—including many Protestants—do not realize that disputes over Christian faith and practice have been present from the beginning. The first major doctrinal dispute concerns Gentile circumcision and the Law of Moses, which was settled by the Apostles and elders at the Council of Jerusalem (Acts 15). We often think only of Arianism (which prompted the Nicene Creed) and then assume the rest was smooth sailing, as if the apostolic faith floated down the centuries untouched. In reality, for over two thousand years, the Church has continually defended, clarified, and handed down what it received from the Apostles.

A good example is the Councils of Carthage in the late fourth and early fifth centuries: the same North African councils that recognized the biblical canon for liturgical use also confronted the moral-theological errors of Pelagianism, which denied the necessity of grace. In other words, the Church that safeguards which books belong in the Bible is the same Church that preserved how those books are to be understood—guarding the apostolic faith in both Scripture and doctrine across all time.

Unlike other heresies, Protestantism was able to succeed where others could not, mainly due to the invention of the printing press, which enabled the rapid and widespread distribution of ideas. This allowed errors to spread faster and further than previous local controversies. Prior heresies stayed relatively local.

Christ's Words About His Church

Here are four verses in which Christ is speaking in His own words, clearly articulating what He has done and what He will do through the Spirit and the Apostles. First, we read: "And I tell you that you are Peter, and on this rock, I will build my church, and the gates of Hades will not overcome it" (Mt 16:18). Those defending the papacy often use this verse to demonstrate Christ's appointment of Peter as the first head of the Church. Protestants tie themselves in knots over what this verse means regarding Peter. I draw attention to the verse with a more straight-forward assertion that Christ established a Church (singular).

To denounce the Catholic claim found in the Nicene Creed, Protestants are left to argue that when Christ says He will build His Church, He is not referring to a visible Church, but rather to the Church established among all believers. Christ, however, is clearly saying He will establish a Church. His Church would be one, holy, catholic, and apostolic.

Christ never wrote anything (as far as we know) and never commanded anyone to write anything. His Church was built on men, apostles whom he instructed orally. When disagreements arose among Christians, Christ taught them how to resolve their differences. Second, we have:

> If your brother or sister sins, go and point out their fault, just between the two of you. If they listen to you, you have won them over. However, if they will not listen, take one or two others along, so that every matter may be established by the testimony of two or three witnesses. If they still refuse to listen, tell it to the church; and if they refuse to listen even to the church, treat them as you would a pagan or a tax collector. (Mt 18:15-17)

This verse from Matthew disproves the Protestant idea that the Church referenced in the Nicene Creed is referencing "all believers." This cannot be the case, since Christ is saying, "Take it to **the** Church."

If this Church is a collection of all believers, then who are they supposed to take it to? Third, we have:

> I have much more to say to you, more than you can now bear. However, when he, the Spirit of truth, comes, he will guide you into all the truth. He will not speak on his own; he will speak only what he hears, and he will tell you what is yet to come. He will glorify me because it is from me that he will receive what he will make known to you. All that belongs to the father is mine. That is why I said the Spirit will receive from me that he will make known to you. (Jn 16:12-15)

In this verse, Christ is explicitly saying that the Spirit will guide the Apostles and has more to share with them, but they are not yet ready. He will reveal more in time. Finally, we read:

> Again, Jesus said, "Peace be with you! As the father has sent me, I am sending you." Moreover, with that, he breathed on them and said, "Receive the Holy Spirit. If you forgive anyone's sins, their sins are forgiven; if you do not forgive them, they are not forgiven." (Jn 20:21-23)

This verse in John is critical, as the only other time God breathed in the Bible was when he breathed life into Adam. Christ breathes life into the church led by the Apostles. John records that Jesus appeared to the Apostles on that first day of the week, said "Peace be with you," breathed on them, and said, "Receive the Holy Spirit." He immediately entrusted them with the ministry of forgiveness: whose sins you forgive are forgiven them.

Early Sunday Worship

Building on how Christ entrusted His Church to the Apostles—commissioning them, promising the Spirit, and sending them to teach—we now see that same apostolic Church gathering each Sunday in a visible pattern of Word and Eucharist from the very beginning. From the first generation, Christians gathered on the first day of the week—the Lord's Day—to "break bread" and devote themselves to "the apostles' teaching, fellowship, and the prayers" (see Acts 2:42). This was not a medieval development but the ordinary life of the Church from the start: Word and Eucharist together in one act of worship.

Very early sources describe the same pattern we know today: Scriptures are read, a homily/exhortation explains them, common prayers are offered, gifts are brought, the Eucharistic thanksgiving is made, the faithful respond "Amen," and Holy Communion is given—followed by a collection for those in need. In other words, the Church's Sunday worship was already apostolic, structured, and sacramental.

What Sunday looked like (apostolic pattern):

- **The Lord's Day:** Christians met on Sunday (not the Jewish Sabbath) to celebrate the Resurrection (see Acts 20:7; 1 Cor 16:2; Rv 1:10).

- **Liturgy of the Word:** Readings from "the Memoirs of the Apostles and the writings of the prophets," with an exhortation/homily explaining their meaning in Christ.

- **Common prayers and peace:** intercessions for the Church and the world; reconciliation/ peace within the assembly.

- **Liturgy of the Eucharist:** bread and wine are presented; the presider gives thanks (*eucharistía*), recalling Christ's words and saving work; the people acclaim "Amen."

- **Holy Communion and collection:** the faithful receive the Eucharist; deacons carry it to the absent; a collection is taken for the poor and widows.

Why this matters:

1. It shows that the Church's worship was visible and communal, not a private Bible study.

2. It confirms Word and Sacrament belong together—not "Bible vs. Church," but Scripture within the Church's worship.

3. It reflects apostolic continuity: bishops, presbyters, and deacons serving a structured liturgy that the whole Church recognized.

4. It demonstrates how unity was established. It provides a mechanism, promised by Christ, to avoid private interpretation.

CHAPTER 2

HOW WE GOT THE BIBLE

Start with Jesus, not a book. Catholics and Protestants alike seldom understand how we got the Bible. When asked, they respond: "God gave it to us." Which, of course, is true. God gave and continues to provide us with everything. However, how did He give it to us? It did not fall from the sky like manna from heaven.

Many do not realize that the Bible is not one book, but a library—a collection of writings composed over many centuries, in different places, by multiple inspired authors, in Hebrew, Aramaic, and Greek. It contains genres (law, history, wisdom, prophecy, Gospels, letters, apocalyptic) written to real communities with real needs. The Old Testament preserves Israel's covenant story; the New Testament records the life of Jesus and the apostolic preaching.

Since the Bible is not a single book but a library of writings gathered into one volume—and it did not fall from heaven neatly bound—it is crucial to know how that collection came to be. Seeing Scripture as a canon of books, not a self-contained rulebook, makes clear why the Church's authority and living Tradition matter for recognizing, preserving, and rightly interpreting it.

To compile, a compiler is needed; someone or some people had to recognize and decide which writings belonged. That is what the early Church did—receiving, reading in worship, and finally establishing the canon so that all Christians would share the same Scriptures. The Bible not only does not tell us which books should be included, but also does not tell us who compiled it.

Not everyone agreed. As the Church spread, some communities were reading texts that were edifying but not ultimately included in the Bible (e.g., the Shepherd of Hermas, the Didache, and 1 Clement). At the same time, some apostolic books were disputed in certain regions. The Church, therefore, had to judge which writings were truly apostolic and consonant with the rule of faith. Regional synods and councils—culminating in notable gatherings, such as those at Rome (382), Hippo (393), and Carthage (397/419)—recognized the canons used in the liturgy and teaching.

Even St. Jerome, who initially favored the narrower Hebrew (Jewish) list for the Old Testament, ultimately deferred to the Church's judgment and included the deuterocanonical books in the Latin Vulgate. In short, because the Bible did not come with its own table of contents, authoritative discernment by the Church was logically necessary to settle genuine disagreements and preserve one Scripture for all.

From Apostolic Preaching to Recognized Canon

- **Apostolic era (first century):** Gospels and letters are written for specific churches, while preaching, sacraments, and discipline are also handed on along with the Gospel. Communities read these texts at worship alongside the Old Testament (often the Septuagint, the Greek Jewish Scriptures used widely by early Christians).

- **Second-third centuries:** Many Christian writings circulate; bishops and churches use criteria like apostolic origin, orthodox teaching, and catholic (universal) usage. By now, there is broad core agreement on most New Testament books, but local differences persist—especially over some letters and the Apocalypse.

- **Council of Rome** (382) under Pope Damasus I: A list matching today's Catholic canon is issued. Pope Damasus also commissions St. Jerome to revise the Latin Gospels, leading to the Vulgate, the standard biblical text of the West for a millennium.

- **Regional Councils of Hippo** (393) and Carthage (397; reaffirmed 419): Reaffirm the same canon for use in the churches of North Africa; Rome's judgment is consulted/ received, strengthening Church-wide consensus.

- **Medieval continuity:** In monasteries and cathedral schools, monks and clerics labor in scriptoria to copy, correct, and preserve biblical manuscripts, often illuminating them by hand. This painstaking work carries Scripture through wars, plagues, and political upheavals.

- **Ecumenical Council of Florence (1442):** Reaffirms the canon in the context of reunion efforts with Eastern Christians.

- **Council of Trent (1546):** In response to Martin Luther and the Reformation disputes (including the status of certain Old Testament books), Trent solemnly defines the canon already received and used in the Church's worship. This is not about "creating" a Bible but instead settling a contested list through the Church's long-standing discernment.

What This Shows

Church → Bible (not Bible → Church). The canon is recognition, not an invention: the Church receives the books that carry apostolic faith and excludes those that do not. Monastic preservation mattered. Without centuries of hand-copying and safeguarding in monasteries (and later universities), much of Scripture would be lost.

The canon was reaffirmed repeatedly. Rome (382), Hippo (393), Carthage (397/419), Florence (1442), and Trent (1546) reaffirm the same list to secure unity in faith and worship across places and centuries. Scripture, therefore, does not and cannot claim to be the only infallible Word of God, as many Protestants claim. Infallible means the inability to make a mistake or commit an error. Fallible and infallible are words that apply to active agents— people make judgments, not inanimate objects like a book.

Humans are ordinarily fallible; sometimes we are right, sometimes wrong. Inanimate objects do not decide. A rock, a plant, or a book does not make judgments. That is why we do not call the Bible "infallible"; the right word is inerrant: everything the Bible asserts, rightly *understood*, is accurate and without error.

The canon we trust directs us to the Church we can see, so the same Church can interpret the Word it recognized. Put simply, the Bible points us to a visible, living authority—the Church, which understands and safeguards the Bible it has received. "The Church of the living God, The pillar and foundation of the truth" (1 Tm 3:15). The Word of God presupposes the people of God; the Bible points to the Church that understands it and urges believers to "hold to the traditions" handed on by word or by letter (2 Thes 2:15). Scripture is inspired; the Church is the Spirit-guided custodian and authentic, authoritative interpreter of that Word, so that the one Gospel is preserved, taught, and lived in unity.

One-Minute Takeaway

The Bible arose within the life of the Church that Jesus founded. Bishops and councils recognized the books already used in apostolic worship; monks preserved them; and the canon was reaffirmed at Rome (382), Hippo (393), Carthage (397/419), Florence (1442), and finally defined at Trent (1546) amid Reformation disputes. The Bible itself never claims to be the only infallible authority; instead, God gave us Scripture within the Church, guarded by the

successors of the Apostles and guided by the Holy
Spirit.

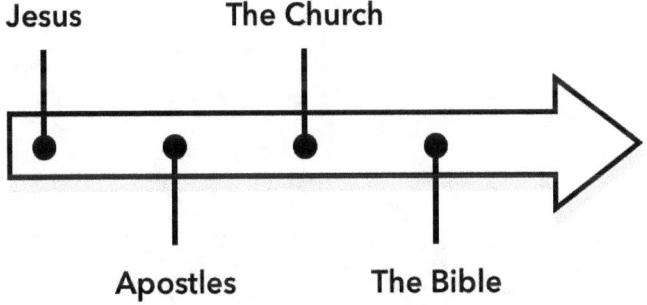

CHAPTER 3

The Logic-Illogic

The Protestant proposition, *Sola Scriptura*—the claim that the Bible is the sole infallible rule of faith—might have an emotional appeal at first glance. We do not need men: we have the book. Men make mistakes, but the book does not. "Just read the book, do not listen to men." However, as we saw in the previous chapter, *Sola Scriptura* is not logically coherent. It cannot explain who recognized the canon, how disputes are finally settled, or why any interpretation should bind others. Emotionally attractive, perhaps; logically insufficient.

When we ask questions—How did we get the book? Who wrote it? Who decided what its contents are? Who decides what it means?—the appeal of *Sola Scriptura* quickly fades. These questions are rarely considered by people who say Catholics are wrong. Worse still, *Sola Scriptura* has led to the proliferation of numerous Christian denominations, all claiming to possess the truth. This is, of course, the expected outcome when interpretation is left to the individual. St. Paul knew as much when he urged Timothy to preach the word faithfully. "For the time is coming when people will not endure sound teaching but, having itching ears, they will accumulate for themselves teachers to suit their own passions, and will turn away from listening to the truth and wander off into myths" (2 Tm 4:3-4).

Many within the Protestant community are beginning to recognize the flaw in their proposition, leaving some to adjust their claim, now saying, "Sola Scriptura does not mean 'Bible alone'; we also value councils and the fathers." However, when pressed, they accept only those councils and Fathers that conform to their private interpretation of the Bible.

That is circular: tradition is treated as authoritative only after it has been pre-approved by the individual reader—authority in name, autonomy in fact. When councils are binding only if I already agree, the final pope is me. Under *Sola Scriptura*, the predictable result has been a never-ending proliferation of denominations, each claiming to teach the truth; whenever a disagreement arises, another church is formed.

By contrast, the Catholic view is not only more straightforward and coherent—it is logical: Scripture is inspired, and the Church Christ founded, guided by the Holy Spirit, serves as the authentic, authoritative interpreter, so that the one Gospel can be preserved, taught, and lived in unity. This not only dispels the illogical Protestant notion that the Church is a confused, invisible body of believers, but also provides the mechanism by which Christ's prayer in John can be realized. "Father, may they be one, as you and I are one" (Jn 17:21).

Common Protestant Elements

Many Protestants deny that Christ intended a perpetuating, sacramental office (bishop/presbyter) to carry binding authority. (Exceptions exist—e.g., some Anglicans and some Lutherans claim succession, but without a universally binding Magisterium.)

- **Sole infallible authority:** Scripture is uniquely God-breathed and therefore the only source that cannot err.

- **Tradition subordinated:** Creeds and councils may help, but they are not binding if they seem to conflict with one's reading of Scripture.

- **No binding Magisterium:** The Church may teach, but no living authority is guaranteed freedom from errors in defining faith and morals.

A Practical Corollary

If *Sola Scriptura* were true, we would still need someone with authority to tell us which books belong in the Bible and how to settle disputes. For Protestants, that is themselves; for Catholics, it is the Church. That is why *Sola Scriptura* defeats itself: the canon and continuity both presuppose the Church. Using the Church guided by the Holy Spirit, as Christ promised, God gave us the Bible.

To deny that Christ established a Spirit-guided Church requires believing that God sent His Son, that Jesus commissioned the Apostles and promised the Spirit, that the Apostles actually taught, and that Christians followed—yet somehow no visible, enduring Church was intended. That collapses the premises and reinterprets Christianity as a matter of private judgment.

Before we engage any objection, notice that our approach is really a simple syllogism—premises that lead to a necessary conclusion. We are not asking anyone to accept a private interpretation; we are asking them to follow basic logic grounded in facts most Christians already affirm.

> **Premise 1**—God sent Jesus: Christianity begins with God's initiative, not human invention.

Premise 2—Jesus teaches and commissions: Jesus taught with authority, chose and commissioned the Apostles, and promised the Holy Spirit to guide them.

Premise 3—The Apostles preach and teach: after the Ascension and Pentecost, the Apostles publicly taught, formed communities, and those Christians followed the Apostles' teaching.

Conclusion—Therefore, Christ established a visible, authoritative Church, guided by the Holy Spirit, to preserve and transmit His teaching across time.

Corollaries (Without Debating Interpretations)

- Scripture belongs within the Church's life; the Church recognized the canon, and a Spirit-guided Church explains continuity of doctrine and visible unity.

- Why "Bible alone" fails the logic test: it needs a table of contents that the Bible does not contain; it presumes the Church's recognition of the canon; it ignores the years when the Gospel was handed on in preaching and worship before a bound New Testament.

- "Bible alone" leads to fragmentation that contradicts Jesus's commissioning and promise of the Spirit to one apostolic body.

If we agree God sent Jesus, that Jesus taught and commissioned the Apostles with the promise of the Holy Spirit, and that the Apostles taught and Christians followed, then the logical conclusion is that Christ established a Spirit-guided Church. The Bible itself belongs inside that Church's life. The "Bible alone" approach breaks the logic because it requires a Church to define what the Bible is.

Which came first: the chicken or the egg? The Church or the Bible?

CHAPTER 4

A THREE-STEP METHOD

Step 1: Agreements

Before addressing the specific claim that Catholics are wrong, start with what most Christians should share. Naming these core truths keeps Christ at the center, provides a common starting point, and lowers defensiveness, allowing trust to grow. It also clarifies the real issue—authority and continuity—instead of sliding into verse-trading.

Jumping straight to Bible duels is like starting a movie halfway through: you miss the plot that makes everything make sense. While almost everyone accepts agreement 1 below, you may be surprised at how many people do not fully grasp agreements 2 and 3 and rely solely on assumptions they have not thoroughly considered.

Agreement 1: God Sent Jesus

God sent Jesus as the fulfillment of His promises—the Word made flesh, the true Lamb, the Son of David, the One in whom the Law and the Prophets find their completion. "God so loved the world that He gave His only begotten Son" (Jn 3:16); "When the fullness of time had come, God sent forth His Son" (Gal 4:4-5).

Agreement 2: Jesus Teaches and Commissions

Jesus taught and commissioned the Apostles, who preached and wrote, and He founded a visible Church, promising that the Holy Spirit would guide it into all truth until the end. "All authority … Go therefore … baptizing … teaching … I am with you always" (Mt 28:18-20); "The Advocate, the Holy Spirit … will teach you all things and remind you of all I told you" (Jn 14:26; see Jn 16:13).

Agreement 3: The Apostles Preach and Teach

The Apostles handed on the faith by word and by letter (2 Thes 2:15), forming communities that gather each Lord's Day for Word and Eucharist (Acts 20:7; 1 Cor 11). They appoint leaders—bishops, presbyters, and deacons—through laying on of hands (Acts 6:6, 14:23; 1 Tm 4:14; 2 Tm 1:6), creating a living chain so the teaching will not die with them: "what you have heard from me … entrust to faithful men who will be able to teach others also" (2 Tm 2:2).

Their letters correct errors, settle disputes (Acts 15), and give a rule of faith that anchors interpretation (e.g., 1 Cor 15:1-5). In short, apostolic preaching is not free-floating talk; it is proclamation, sacramental life, and authorized oversight—a pattern designed to preserve, explain, and transmit Christ's teaching to every generation.

For many, the story stops at "Jesus died and rose." They are aware that the Apostles existed and that their writings comprise the New Testament, but they rarely delve further. In reality, the Apostles did not merely write a few letters; they preached, taught, traveled, corrected errors, founded churches, and established structures. Jesus' resurrection is the beginning of his Church.

After the Resurrection and Pentecost, the Apostles did exactly what Jesus commanded: they preached the Gospel publicly and taught the Church continually. Peter's Pentecost sermon announces Jesus as crucified and risen (Acts 2); thousands are baptized, and the new believers "devoted themselves to the apostles' teaching and fellowship, to the breaking of the bread and the prayers" (Acts 2:42).

They handed on the faith "by word and by letter," gathered believers each Lord's Day for Word and Eucharist, and appointed leaders—bishops, presbyters, and deacons—by the laying on of hands so the Gospel would not die with the first generation. The apostles consistently used the **laying on of hands** to commission leaders—an Old Testament sign of real authority being passed on.

> *"They presented these men to the apostles, who prayed and laid their hands on them."* (Acts 6:6)

This wasn't symbolic encouragement. It was a **public act of authorization**. That living chain is visible in concrete lines of succession: John formed Polycarp of Smyrna, and Polycarp formed Irenaeus of Lyons. In other words, the New Testament did not create the Church; instead, the Church's apostolic life created, preserved, and authentically handed down the New Testament—and continued to teach it in every generation.

Try to find agreement on at least one of these. Number one is the easiest because it is the most well-known. Numbers two and three are less understood but important, as they demonstrate how the church was established and grew. You should have a solid understanding of all three so that you can return to them later when discussing step 3 of the method.

Read Acts straight through and the formation of the Church is unmistakable: the Apostles' teaching and fellowship, the breaking of the bread and the prayers, deacons and presbyters appointed, bishops emerging in key cities, a universal decision at the Jerusalem Council, Sunday gatherings, and an ordered mission that carries the Gospel to the nations. When we consider not only what was written but also what was done, the picture becomes clearer.

After you establish at least one agreement, move on to step two.

Step 2: Ask "Why" or "How" and Clarify Assumptions

One reason we get rattled when we hear "Catholics are wrong" is that we feel put on the defensive.

Maybe you do not know why we confess our sins to a priest (you should, and you can learn). If you do not, it is okay—you are still following Christ by doing it. Nevertheless, when someone presses you, that uncertainty can feel like guilt, and guilt quickly turns into defensiveness. Even if you answer well, you will often be hit with a flurry of claims, and eventually, one that you cannot address on the spot.

Instead, ask first: "Why do you think that is wrong?" or "Where did you hear that?" The goal is not to chase every issue; it is to help them notice the assumptions underneath their claim. Do not tell them they have a false assumption—that shuts people down. Help them discover it for themselves. Once they see the shaky foundation (for example, that the Bible somehow chose its own books, or that all "tradition" is bad), the rest of the objections start to wobble with it. Then the specific "Catholics are wrong about X" no longer matters because the foundation they were standing on was not solid.

They may raise good questions, so listen carefully and stay humble. Every challenge is an opportunity to deepen your faith. However, when someone says, "Catholics are wrong," you aim to let them own their claim—slow down, explain where it came from, and think through the logic. That simple shift moves the burden of proof back where it belongs and opens the door to a calmer, more honest conversation.

Primary Question

"Can I ask, *why* do you think that [X] is wrong?" Replace [X] with the specific claim (e.g., papacy, confession, Eucharist, tradition). It does not matter what they claim.

Variations (Same Intent)

"Who or where did you learn that [X] is wrong?" "What assumptions are you making?"

"How do you know that is true?" "Is it possible you might be wrong?" "What source should I look at to understand your view on [X]?" "Is there a book, video, church, or teacher you rely on for [X]?"

Handle the Answer (No Debate Yet)

Listen completely; do not interrupt.

The Bible Says ↷ No, It Doesn't

"If they still refuse to listen, tell it to the **Church**; and if they refuse to listen even to the Church, treat them as you would a pagan or a tax collector."

- Matthew 18:15-17

Step 3: Authority

Since it is their sole infallible authority, when asked *how or why* they know Catholics are wrong, the Protestant relies on the Bible. Moreover, they are relying on their interpretation of the Bible. Since sincere Christians can come to different understandings, or even not fully understand a passage, Protestants are in the position of making themselves the authority. Asking the question, "How do you know that?" will begin to draw them into the reality that they are relying on themselves for their understanding. Next, ask, "By what *authority* do you trust the Bible?"

A Note on Harmony

"Be not afraid." Your interlocutor may fire a Bible verse that appears to oppose Church teaching. Properly read in context and within the Church that recognized the canon, no verse of Scripture contradicts Catholic doctrine. Verse duels arise when texts are isolated from the Church's living rule of faith, or when someone reads into the text. Reading *into* a text is eisegesis (imposing your ideas onto it). The opposite is exegesis—drawing the author's intended meaning *out of* the text by attending to context, genre, language, historical setting, and the text's own flow.

For example, when a Protestant says a Catholic is wrong for calling a priest father, they often point to this Bible verse: "And do not call anyone on earth 'father,' for you have one Father, and he is in heaven" (Mt 23:9). In order to show that the Catholic Church is wrong, the protestant uses the verse in isolation, reading into it (eisegesis) as a literal ban on calling anyone on earth "father." In the New Testament, there are numerous instances of spiritual father language, as seen in Paul's use of the phrase, "I became your father in Christ" (1 Cor 4:15), and his description of Timothy as his "true child" (1 Tm 1:2). When read as the author intended, we see the prohibition targets vainglory, rather than the reality of spiritual fatherhood.

Jesus is condemning Pharisaic vanity. This eise-gesis is so blatantly obvious that most Protestants stopped using it.

So next time someone answers "The Bible says ...," respond calmly: "I love Scripture. Could we reflect on how we came to have the Bible? Then we can look at your verse in that light."

The Short Story (Shared Facts)

- Jesus founded a Church, not a book; He chose Apostles whom He taught, promised the Holy Spirit would be with them, and sent them on a mission.

- The Apostles first preached and taught; the Gospel was handed on by word in worship and daily life.

- Some apostolic teaching was written; Gospels and letters were read in the liturgy alongside the Old Testament.

- Many Christian writings circulated; the Church used criteria such as apostolicity, orthodoxy, and catholicity (wideness) of usage.

- Local and regional councils listed the same books; the Church reaffirmed this canon used in worship.

- Therefore, appeals to "The Bible says …" presuppose the Church that recognized the Bible. The Bible and the Church are not rivals.

Why Ask Questions? (Socratic Method in Apologetics)

Asking *why* questions—at the heart of the Socratic method—slows a conversation down in the best possible way. Instead of debating conclusions, it invites people to examine the assumptions beneath them. A well-timed *why* doesn't accuse or corner; it opens space for reflection, clarity, and mutual understanding. In dialogue, this shifts the tone from winning an argument to discovering truth together, helping people articulate their reasoning, notice gaps or inconsistencies, and often arrive at deeper insight on their own.

Here is an example of the Socratic method in action:

> **You:** Have you read the Gospel of Thomas? What about The Epistle of Barnabas? Or the Acts of Paul and Thecla? What about the Gospel of Peter?
>
> **Friend:** No.
>
> **You:** How come?

Friend: They are not in the Bible.

You: Why not?

Friend: I do not know. I never heard of them.

You: That is precisely my point. Someone had to decide which books belong—the Bible does not list its own table of contents.

Friend: Huh, I never thought about that.

You: Early Christians used a vast number of writings. The Church recognized the ones truly tied to the Apostles, consistently used in worship, and faithful to the rule of faith.

Friend: So, the Church picked the books?

You: Better word: recognized. They did not invent Scripture; they discerned what God had inspired—at councils such as Rome (382) and Carthage (397/419)—so that all Christians would read the same New Testament.

Friend: Okay, but what about interpretation?

You: Same pattern. The Bible came through the Church, and Scripture is read within the Church that received it. That is why jumping straight to "my interpretation vs. yours" does not work.

Notice in that sample dialogue, I made very few assertive statements. Instead, I asked questions—the Socratic approach. This is not a trick; it is a way to help someone discover truth rather than feel pushed into it.

Remember, many people, including Catholics, think the Bible is one big book. It is not. The Bible is a library—a collection of different writings composed over centuries, in various places, and in multiple genres (law, history, wisdom, prophecy, Gospels, letters, and more).

Why do questions work:

- **Lower defensiveness:** Questions feel safe; they invite reflection instead of triggering a fight-or-flight response.

- **Surface assumptions:** People often stand on unspoken premises (e.g., "the Bible chose itself"). Questions bring those premises into the light.

- **Build trust:** You show genuine interest in the person, not just in winning.

- **Teaches how to think, not what to think:** your friend learns to trace the logic (Jesus → Apostles → Church → Canon) for themselves.

How to use it (practical steps):

- Start with shared ground. "Can we agree God sent Jesus; Jesus taught and commissioned; the Apostles preached and taught?"

- Ask clarifying questions. "Who/where did you learn that X is wrong?"

- Probe the canon fact. "How do we know which books belong in the Bible if the Bible does not list them?"

- Ask about origins. "Do you know how God gave us the Bible?"

- Connect the dots. "If the Church recognized the canon, where should we look when interpretations conflict?"

- Invite a small next step. "Would you read one short page and then come to Mass with me?"

Sample Socratic prompts you can reuse.

- "What would count as good evidence for you?"

- "How do you know that is true?"

- "What assumptions are you making?"

- "If two sincere Christians disagree, who decides—on what authority?"

- "How did the earliest Christians worship before there was a bound New Testament?"
- "If the Bible is the only infallible authority, how did we get the Bible without a Church?"
- "When Jesus said, 'tell it to the Church' (Mt 18:17), what did He expect us to do in real disputes?"

Do / Do not!

- Do listen, reflect, and ask one straightforward question at a time.
- Do aim for small wins (one truth at a time), not a knockout blow.
- Do not jump into verse duels—keep the focus on structure and authority.
- Do not interrogate; keep a warm tone and let them think.

One-line summary:

Good questions open doors; logic alone cannot. The Socratic path lets your friend see that the same Christ who gave us Scripture also gave us the Church—so objections can be faced on a solid foundation.

Quick Timeline Refresher

- Jesus → the Apostles (Church)

- Apostles → preach/teach; communities worship

- Texts → letters and Gospels for those communities

- Discernment → which writings are truly apostolic and orthodox

- Canon → Church recognizes the list used in worship

- Today → we read the Bible in the Church

CHAPTER 5

THE BIBLE AND INTERPRETATION

Resist the reflex to debate. When a Protestant says, "The Bible says …," he really means his interpretation of the Bible or what he may have learned from someone else. Of course, the Apostles knew this would happen. Paul, in his final letter to Timothy, writes: "The time will come when men will not put up with sound doctrine. Instead, to suit their own desires, they will gather around them a great number of teachers to say what their itching ears want to hear" (2 Tm 4:3).

You might be tempted to start answering the objection or jumping into interpretation. Do not. You do not need to. All you will do is go around in circles. Many times, I have demonstrated to the Protestant that his interpretation was wrong, only for him to jump to another argument.

Keep the conversation on Christ's structure—Jesus → Apostles → Church—and ask for sources. Remember, this is not about verse picking; it is about establishing authority. Authority resides in the Church that Christ founded, not in a private reading contest.

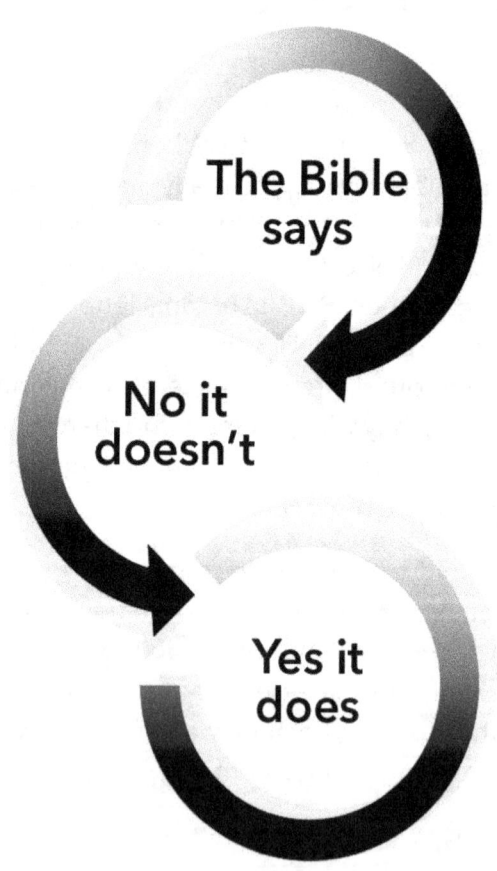

The Problem with Interpretation Fights

- Everyone has a verse; proof-text exchanges can go forever and go nowhere.

- Sincere Christians reach opposite conclusions, each saying "the Bible says."

- This is not how Jesus set it up: He founded a Church, taught, commissioned, and promised the Spirit to guide the Apostles. *"Take it to the Church."*

Keep the Conversation Fruitful

- Name the trap: "I do not think a duel of interpretations will help either of us."

- Re-center on agreements: God sent Jesus; Jesus teaches and commissions; Apostles preach and teach.

- Stay with Jesus → Apostles → Church before meanings.

- Ask for the source (step 2).

- Recall the canon fact: the Church recognized Scripture; let us hear Scripture within that Church.

Even Peter warns: "His letters contain some things that are hard to understand, which ignorant and unstable people distort, as they do the other Scriptures, to their own destruction" (2 Pt 3:16).

It is for this very reason that I will often go as far as saying something like, "I do not care what you think the verse means; quite frankly, I do not care what I think it means; I only care about what God means."

I am not sure about you, but I make mistakes all the time. Jesus knew this, which is why He promised that the Holy Spirit would guide His *Church*. There has to be a supernatural authority.

CHAPTER 6

APPLYING THE FRAMEWORK

Use the same sequence every time:

Agreements → Ask How/Why → Authority, Canon, Fact → Christ's Structure.

The Four-Move Script

- **Restate** agreements.

- **Ask:** "Says Who?" "Who/where did you learn that [X] is wrong?" "How do you know that is true?"

- **Authority:** Jesus founded a Church; Apostles handed it down; the Church recognized the canon.

- **Christ's Structure:** look at what Jesus said and did, what the Apostles handed on, how the earliest Church lived.

Boundaries

- Decline verse duels.

- One topic at a time; one shared source; don't monopolize the conversation.

- Close with peace: "I am seeking truth with you, not points against you."

Openers

- "Could we start with what we agree on, then take your concern one step at a time?"

- "To avoid an interpretation duel, let us begin with Jesus and the Apostles."

Key Bible Verses

You do not need to memorize the entire Bible nor be able to cite chapter and verse, but you should be familiar with some key verses. Often, when I talk with Catholics, they express some embarrassment about not being able to recite a Bible passage with chapter and verse. It is worth knowing that the Bible, when originally written, did not have chapters and verse numbers. Modern chapter divisions were introduced in the thirteenth century, and verse numbers in the sixteenth century.

Remember: even Satan can quote the Bible. In the wilderness, he cited Scripture to tempt Jesus (see Mt 4:1–11; Lk 4:1–13). Christ answered with

Scripture in its true sense—within the obedience of faith—not as proof-texts for self-will. That is why Christians need Scripture within the Church's living faith, not verses torn from context. Here are a few important verses that you should know.

> **John 3:16:** "For God so loved the world that he gave his only Son, that whoever believes in him should not perish but have eternal life."

> **Galatians 4:4-5:** "When the fullness of time had come, God sent forth his Son … to redeem those who were under the law, so that we might receive adoption as sons."

> **Matthew 28:18-20:** "All authority in heaven and on earth has been given to me. Go therefore and make disciples … baptizing … teaching … and behold, I am with you always, to the close of the age."

> **John 14:26:** "The Helper, the Holy Spirit … will teach you all things and bring to your remembrance all that I have said to you."

> **John 16:13:** "When the Spirit of truth comes, he will guide you into all the truth …"

> **Acts 2:42:** "They devoted themselves to the apostles' teaching and fellowship, to the breaking of the bread and the prayers."

> **2 Thessalonians 2:15:** "Stand firm and hold to the traditions which you were taught by us, either by word of mouth or by letter."

> **2 Timothy 2:2:** "What you have heard from me … entrust to faithful men who will be able to teach others also."

Notice that in none of these, nor in any verse in the Bible, does it say God sent His Son, then He sent a book. His son gathered men, imperfect men, whom He taught and promised that He *breathed* on them.

Jesus breathed on His Apostles and gave them the Holy Spirit on the night of His Resurrection, in the Upper Room, as described in John 20:22, an event that was a prophetic precursor to the descent of the Holy Spirit at Pentecost. This event empowered them to forgive sins. It marked the beginning of the Church, which was fully established fifty days later with the mighty outpouring of the Holy Spirit on Pentecost. The only other time God breathed is when He breathed life into Adam: "Then the Lord God formed a man from the dust of the ground and breathed into his nostrils the breath of life, and the man became a living being" (Gn 2:7).

CHAPTER 7

MOTIVES OF CREDIBILITY—WHY THE CHURCH'S VERY EXISTENCE POINTS TO DIVINE ORIGIN

Christians are not asked to make a blind leap. From the beginning, God has accompanied His revelation with public signs that make faith reasonable. Classical theology calls these signs *motives of credibility*—clues strong enough to show that God has spoken and that the community guarding that word is not merely human.

Miracles and Prophecy (Then and Now)

In Scripture, God authenticates His messengers by deeds only He can do (the Exodus, Elijah's fire, Christ's healings, and the Resurrection). Prophecy likewise credentials revelation (Messiah foretold; the Church foreshadowed as a kingdom that endures). These are not private experiences, but public facts tied to history and witnesses.

The Church herself is an ongoing sign:

Vatican I (echoed in the Catechism) teaches that the Church's growth, holiness, fruitfulness, unity, universality, and stability are themselves a standing motive of credibility—evidence that something more than human organization is at work. In plain terms: kingdoms rise and fall, philosophies flare and fade, but the one, holy, catholic, and apostolic Church endures across languages, continents, and centuries—still teaching one Creed, celebrating one Eucharist, and tracing one apostolic line. That "improbable durability" is precisely the sort of sign we would expect if Christ truly promised, "the gates of hell shall not prevail."

Continuity through persecution and cultural upheaval:

From the Roman persecutions to medieval plagues, from schisms and reform to modern totalitarian regimes, the Church has been pressed on every side—yet she survives and rebounds, often becoming spiritually stronger after crises. As St. Augustine argued, the rapid conversion of nations by a handful of humble preachers, despite hostility, is either the work of God or a greater miracle still if it happened without Him. Either way, the Church's rise and endurance function as public proof of her divine mission.

Sanctity and beauty as credible signs:

Holiness is not an abstraction: it is visible in the saints, in sacrificial love, in institutions of mercy, in the luminous coherence of Christian moral teaching. Beauty, too, "wounds" us toward God—think of the Gospel's moral splendor, the liturgy's nobility, the arts faith has inspired. These are not *the* argument, but they are powerful "fittings" that make the claim of divine origin morally compelling.

What About Scandals?

Sinners in the Church do not disprove her holiness any more than traitors disprove a nation's ideals. Immorality is explainable by merely human weakness; heroic sanctity is not. The Church explicitly condemns the sins of her members, calls them to repentance, and canonizes those who live the Gospel—another sign that her life-source exceeds human effort.

What Does This Prove?

Motives of credibility do not compel faith; they undermine the claim that faith is irrational.

They show that trusting Christ—and the Church He founded—fits the facts. If God truly revealed Himself in Jesus, it makes sense that He would also provide a visible community that preserves, teaches, and sacramentally communicates that revelation across time. The Church's two-millennia continuity, unity-in-catholicity, and persistent fruitfulness are precisely the sort of public, testable signs that anchor divine claims in history.

Summary

Miracles and prophecy began the story; the Church's enduring, holy, worldwide life continues it—standing, generation after generation, as a credible sign that her origin is not merely human but divine.

Each one claims to teach the Bible correctly, yet they contradict one another on topics such as baptism, the Eucharist, authority, moral teaching, and even salvation itself. This fragmentation is not proof that Scripture fails; rather, it is what happens when there is no living, binding authority to settle disputes. By contrast, the one Church that compiled the canon has endured in unity of faith and sacraments.

What follows is a brief list of denominations, their date of founding, their founders, and their place of founding—a snapshot of how, despite claiming the Bible alone, competing interpretations multiply when there is no final arbiter.

Divisions

Catholic
Jerusalem, 33

Jesus Christ

Orthodox
Constantinople, 1054

Schismatic Catholic bishops

Lutheran
Germany, 1517

Martin Luther

Anabaptist
Germany, 1512

Nicholas Storch & Thomas Munzer

Anglican
England, 1534

Henry VIII

Mennonites
Switzerland, 1536

Menno Simons

Calvinist
Switzerland, 1555

John Calvin

Presbyterian
Scotland, 1560

John Knox

Congregational
Holland, 1582

Robert Brown

Baptist *Amsterdam, 1609*	John Smyth
Dutch Reformed *New York, 1628*	Michaelis Jones
Congregationalist *Massachusetts, 1648*	Pilgrims and Puritans
Quakers *England, 1649*	George Fox
Amish *France, 1693*	Jacob Amman
Freemasons *London, 1717*	Masons from four lodges
Methodist *England, 1739*	John and Charles Wesley
Unitarian *London, 1774*	Theophilus Lindey
Methodist Episcopal *Baltimore, Maryland, 1784*	Sixty Preachers
Episcopalian *American Colonies, 1789*	Samuel Seabury

United Brethren *Maryland, 1800*	Philip Otterbein and Martin Boehn
Disciples of Christ *Kentucky, 1827*	Thomas and Alexander Campbell
Mormon *New York, 1830*	Joseph Smith
Methodist Protestant *United States, 1830*	Methodist
Church of Christ *Kentucky, 1836*	Warren Stone & Alexander Campbell
Seventh-day Adventist *Washington,* *New Hampshire, 1844*	Ellen White
Christadelphian **(Brethren of Christ)** *Richmond, Virginia, 1844*	John Thomas
Salvation Army *London, 1865*	William Booth
Holiness *United States, 1867*	Methodist
Jehovah's Witnesses *Pennsylvania, 1874*	Charles Taze Russell

Christian Science *Boston, 1879*	Mary Baker Eddy
Church of God in Christ *Arkansas, 1895*	Various churches of God
Church of Nazarene *Pilot Point, TX, c.1850-1900*	Various religious bodies
Pentecostal *Topeka, Kansas, 1901*	Charles F. Parkham
Aglipayan *Philippines, 1902*	Gregorio Aglipay
Assemblies of God *Hot Springs, Arizona, 1914*	Pentecostalism
Iglesia ni Christo *Philippines, 1914*	Felix Manalo
Four-square Gospel *Los Angeles, CA, 1917*	Aimee Semple McPherson
United Church of Christ *Philadelphia, PA, 1961*	Reformed and Congregationalist
Calvary Chapel *Costa Mesa, CA, 1965*	Chuck Smith

United Methodist *Dallas, Texas, 1968*	Methodist and United Brethren
Born-again *United States, c.1970s*	Various religious bodies
Harvest Christian *Riverside, California, 1972*	Greg Laurie
Saddleback *California, 1982*	Rick Warren
Non-denominational *United States, c.1990s*	Various

CHAPTER 8

A Personal Relationship with Christ—In the Heart of His Church

Conversation

In all my years talking with and debating Protestants, I have never met someone who—after reading the Bible entirely on their own—concluded that the Catholic Church is wrong. I have met many sincere Protestants (often former Catholics) who were *taught* that the Church is wrong by a persuasive preacher, a friend, or a community they came to trust, and then found verses in the Bible that seemed to support their view.

Many times, a lapsed Catholic hears about Jesus from a co-worker or neighbor, and because God has planted in every human heart a longing for Himself, that person responds. They want to return to a living relationship with Christ. The Protestant message frequently emphasizes an emotional invitation and rightly highlights the importance of a personal relationship with Jesus—something the Catholic Church not only affirms but insists upon.

A Common Scenario

Maria drifted from the Church during college. Years later, her co-worker Hannah invites her to a midweek Bible study. Maria feels welcomed, hears Scripture explained in a way that speaks to her life, and senses God addressing her heart. On Sunday, she visits Hannah's church. The pastor offers an altar call: "If you want to know Jesus personally, come forward." Moved to tears, Maria steps forward and prays sincerely, telling God she wants to belong to Him. In that moment, authentic grace is at work—God drawing a soul to Himself.

From a Catholic perspective, what Maria longs for is precisely what is right: a living friendship with Jesus. However, the next step is not to pit that relationship against the Church, but to bring it into its fullness—through the Scriptures proclaimed in the liturgy, the forgiveness Christ breathed on the Apostles in the Sacrament of Confession, and the Eucharist, where He gives us His very self. The

Church is not the rival of a personal relationship with Christ—it is the place Christ established for that relationship to be nourished, healed, and sustained.

Over time, Maria encountered many sincere Christians. Each loved Jesus. Each quoted Scripture. And each seemed confident—until they disagreed.

One friend told her that divorce was always wrong. Another said that God understood if a marriage no longer "bore fruit." One said sex with her boyfriend was sinful; another assured her that love mattered more than rules. Some insisted Sunday worship was essential; others said church attendance was optional—*"God doesn't care where you are, as long as your heart is right."*

None of these friends were malicious. None were trying to mislead her. They were thoughtful, prayerful people doing their best to follow Christ. But Maria began to notice something unsettling: **the answers changed depending on who she asked**.

Even more striking, when disagreements grew uncomfortable, people didn't wrestle them out— they left. They changed churches. Or started home groups. Or quietly stopped attending altogether. Each move was justified the same way: *"I just don't feel right there anymore."*

Maria's conscience began to stir. *Is this really how truth works?* she wondered. *If Scripture is clear, why do we keep disagreeing? And if everyone is sincere, how do I know who is right?*

Without meaning to, Maria found herself becoming the final referee. She weighed sermons. She compared interpretations. She evaluated moral claims. She decided which teachings felt reasonable and which felt "too much." The faith she lived by was personal—but also precarious. Everything depended on her judgment, her clarity, her confidence. Then she met someone Catholic.

At first, Maria dismissed the idea outright. One thing all her Christian friends—despite their many disagreements—*did* agree on was this: **Catholics are wrong**. Wrong about authority. Wrong about sacraments. Wrong about Mary. Wrong about "rules."

But her Catholic friend didn't argue the way Maria expected. She didn't trade verses or attack other Christians. Instead, she asked a simple question: "Do you ever get tired of having to decide everything yourself?" The question lingered. Eventually, Maria returned to a Catholic Mass—not out of nostalgia, but out of fatigue. She wanted faith that did not require her to be the final referee. What struck her immediately was not emotion, but structure. Scripture was proclaimed, not debated.

The Creed was recited, not negotiated. The prayers were not spontaneous reflections, but inherited words—received, not invented.

No one asked for Maria's interpretation of the Gospel. The Church simply handed it on.

For the first time in years, Maria felt relieved of a burden she hadn't realized she was carrying: **the burden of deciding everything herself**. She began to grasp something fundamental. Catholicism does not ask the believer to generate certainty from within. It asks the believer to *receive* what Christ entrusted to the Church. The same Church that preserved the Scriptures, recognized the canon, and safeguarded the faith through centuries of disagreement, had not suddenly become unnecessary once the Bible was compiled.

Here, authority was not arbitrary. It was continuous. When Maria went to Confession, the difference became unmistakable. Forgiveness was not inferred from her sincerity; it was declared. She did not have to analyze whether she had repented "enough" or felt the right emotion. Christ's mercy was spoken authoritatively—because Christ had actually given His Church the authority to bind and loose. And in the Eucharist, the contrast reached its clearest point.

In many Protestant settings, communion points backward—a reminder of what Jesus did. In the Catholic Church, it points forward and outward—Christ acting *now*, feeding His people, sustaining them objectively, whether they feel spiritually strong or not.

Maria realized that the Catholic Church was not competing with a "personal relationship with Jesus." It was refusing to reduce that relationship to feelings, interpretations, or private judgments. It insisted that if Christ truly entered history, then He also established a visible, enduring way for real people—confused, sinful, inconsistent people—to remain in communion with Him across time.

The Protestant model Maria had lived by was sincere—but fragile. It depended on internal certainty. When confidence was high, faith felt strong. When confidence wavered, everything wavered with it. The Catholic model was harder—but steadier. It asked for less of her emotions and more of her trust. Not trust in herself, but trust that Christ knew what He was doing when He built a Church, appointed Apostles, and promised the Spirit would guide her.

Eventually, Maria said to Hannah—gently, without accusation: "I'm grateful you invited me. God used that. But I needed more than inspiration. I needed a place where truth doesn't reset every generation, where forgiveness isn't guessed at, and where Scripture isn't severed from the authority that gave it to us."

That is the Catholic claim in its simplest form. Not that Catholics are better Christians. Not that Protestants are insincere. But Christ did not leave His followers alone with a book and their own conclusions. He left the Church.

A Church that nourishes faith through Scripture proclaimed in worship. A Church that heals through real authority to forgive sins. A Church that sustains communion through the Eucharist—Christ Himself, given again and again. So when someone says, *"Catholics are wrong,"* the response need not be defensive. It can be calm—even gentle:

"Wrong about what—and according to whose authority?"

Because once that question is asked honestly, the issue is no longer Catholic versus Protestant. It is Christ's Church—or everyone on their own.

Practical Bridge: From "Altar Call" to the Altar of the Eucharist

- **Affirm the grace:** "Your desire to know Jesus is beautiful. Hold onto that desire."

- **Invite the fullness:** "Come and see how Christians worshiped from the beginning: Word *and* Eucharist."

- **Offer a next step:** "Let us go to Mass this Sunday. I will sit with you and answer questions after."

- **Reconciliation as a gift:** "If you would like, we can also talk to a priest about Confession so you can experience the mercy Jesus promised."

The Psychology of Faith Conversations

Most people do not change their minds because of a single airtight argument. They change when truth and trust arrive together—and both are easily disrupted by emotion. When a long-held belief is challenged, the brain often goes into threat mode: heart rate rises, attention narrows, and we defend our identity rather than evaluate new information. Recognizing this dynamic helps you maintain conversations that are both fruitful and kind.

What is happening inside:

- **Identity attachment:** Beliefs are tied to belonging—family, friends, a beloved pastor. A challenge can feel like a threat to relationships, not just ideas.

- **Confirmation reflex:** Under emotional load, we instinctively favor data that agree with us and discount what does not.

- **Cognitive overload:** Too much information, too fast, triggers shutdown or defensiveness.

- **Social risk:** Admitting "I might be wrong" can feel like losing face in a community we love.

How to Keep the Temperature Low

1. **Lead with shared ground:** "We both love Jesus and want to follow Him." This signals safety.

2. **Ask before you answer:** "Who helped you understand this? What would change your mind?" Questions reduce threat and invite reflection.

3. **Go slow—one pebble at a time:** offer one clear point, not ten. Let silence do work.

4. **Name the emotion, not just the logic:** "I get why this is sensitive—it touches your pastor's teaching and your family's story."

5. **Acknowledge cost:** conversion costs something. Respect that. "No pressure—truth does not fear time."

6. **Use stories and practices, not only proofs:** "Come to Mass with me. Listen. No commitments—just experience."

7. **Exit without closing the door:** "Thanks for trusting me with your questions. Want to read one short page and talk again next week?"

A Quick Reset When Things Get Heated

"I really respect your love for Jesus. I do not want this to become a win-lose. Could we pause the back-and-forth and examine how the earliest Christians actually lived in relation to the Word and Eucharist, the Apostles, and the Church? If that is fair, I will go slow."

Mini-Script: Personal Relationship *Within* the Church

- **You:** "Can we agree God sent Jesus, Jesus taught and commissioned the Apostles, and the Apostles preached and taught?"

- **Friend:** "Yes."

- **You:** "Great. Then the question is where Jesus intends that relationship to grow. From the beginning, Christians gathered on Sunday for the Word and the Eucharist, living under the guidance of apostolic shepherds. The same Church that recognizes the Bible also teaches how to live it. Would you come and see?"

Reflection Questions

1. When someone challenges your faith, which emotions rise first? How do those emotions shape your response?

2. Who first taught **you** about a personal relationship with Jesus? How has the Church deepened that relationship?

3. What small step could you invite a friend to take this week—Mass, Confession, coffee with a priest, or reading one page together?

Quick Send-Off

Hold onto the relationship and invite fullness. Honor the grace that awakens a heart to Jesus— and gently lead that heart into the Church where Jesus has continuously fed, forgiven, and formed His people. From a Catholic perspective, what Maria desires is exactly right: a living friendship with Jesus. The next step is to bring that relationship into the fullness of the life Christ gave His Church—the Scriptures proclaimed in the liturgy, the forgiveness Jesus breathed upon the Apostles, and the Eucharist that unites us to Him. Rather than pitting a "personal relationship with Christ" against the Church, we can show how the Church is precisely where that relationship is nourished, healed, and sustained by the means Christ established.

Why Foundations Matter in Handling Objections

When a Catholic faces a disagreement, the next step is to "tell it to the Church" (Mt 18:17)—to appeal to the living authority Christ entrusted to the Apostles and their successors. When a Protestant faces a disagreement, the typical pattern is to seek another church or start a new one, because no one is recognized as a binding, final arbiter. That is why handling objections without an agreed foundation is impossible: if no authority can finally say what the faith means, every dispute is reduced to private judgment. In practice, the Protestant stance often (even if unintentionally) makes the individual the final authority. This is not mere opinion; it is the logic of the structure.

The logic in three steps:

1. If Scripture alone is the sole infallible rule and no living authority is binding,

2. Then each interpreter (or voluntary group) becomes the final judge of what Scripture means,

3. Therefore, disputes can only end by separating—not by submitting to a shared, visible authority.

Catholic (Universal) Alternative:

Christ established a visible Church with teaching authority (Jesus → Apostles → successors), so that the true faith could be passed down and disagreements could be resolved within the communion He founded, rather than multiplying into new communions.

> *If I don't agree with my Pastor, I find another Pastor. —Charlie Kirk*

The Night It Clicked

A close friend of mine married a kind, energetic "born-again" Christian woman. She truly loved Jesus—and she truly loved telling me that Catholics are wrong. Every visit followed the same routine: she'd launch an objection, I'd answer with Scripture and basic logic, and she'd pivot to another point. It felt like theological whack-a-mole. Sometimes I had the response on the tip of my tongue; other times, I had to do research and follow up by email. No matter how many objections I addressed, she never accepted the answers; she just jumped to the next.

Eventually, we agreed to stop debating. "We both love Christ," we said. "Let's just leave it there."

Months later, I visited their home one evening. Conversation was light, the kids were playing, and then—there it was again: "You know Catholics are wrong about ___." I felt that inner sigh. We'd been down this road. I didn't want another circular sparring match. A priest friend's advice came back to me. Fr. Paul taught me the one-second prayer. Whenever you are stuck and not sure what to say, pray, "Come, Holy Spirit." So, quietly, I prayed, and instead of launching into proof texts, I asked a question.

"Have you ever read the Gospel of Thomas?"

She blinked. "No."

"Why not?"

"There is no Gospel of Thomas," she said.

"Yes, there is," I replied. "It's often called a 'lost gospel.' Hollywood loves to dramatize it."

"Oh—well, it's not biblical."

"How do you know?" I asked. "Have you read it?"

"No."

"Why not?"

"It's not in the Bible," she replied.

"So you haven't read it because it's not in the Bible," I said slowly, "and you know it doesn't belong in the Bible because it's not in the Bible."

She hesitated. "Well … the Bible is all we need."

I nodded. "That's exactly the problem. You're using the Bible to justify the Bible—without ever asking how the Bible came to be the Bible."

I continued. "There are other early Christian writings—the Epistle of Barnabas, the Acts of Paul and Thecla, the Gospel of Peter. Have you read any of them?"

"No. They're not in the Bible."

"Right," I said. "And you haven't read them because they're not in the Bible, and you know they don't belong in the Bible because you haven't read them. That's circular reasoning."

She shifted uncomfortably.

"You say, 'All I need is the Bible,'" I went on, "but you've never asked who decided which books would count as the Bible in the first place. The Bible doesn't contain a table of contents inspired by God. It didn't fall from heaven, leather-bound with gold-edged pages."

"For centuries," I continued, "Christians heard the Gospel preached, worshiped in the Church, and received teaching long before the New Testament was formally gathered. There were real disagreements, real debates, and real decisions made by the Church about what was apostolic and what wasn't."

She nodded, but cautiously now.

"Let me press this a little further," I said. "Try an experiment."

"Suppose you, your husband, and I all open our Bibles to the same passage. We're all sincere. We all know how to read. We all pray for the Holy Spirit."

"Your husband reads it and says it means X. I read it and say it means Y. You read it and say it means Z."

"Now here's the key question: who decides?"

She didn't answer.

"Because what you're actually saying," I continued, "is that your interpretation is the correct one—and that your husband, me, and every Christian who disagrees with you is wrong."

She frowned. "When you say it like that, it sounds arrogant."

"It's not about intention," I said. "It's about authority. In practice, the individual becomes the final judge–sitting above Scripture, above history, and above the Church Christ founded."

The room went quiet.

I didn't rush to fill it.

"Before we start trading verses again," I said finally, "we need to answer a more fundamental question: did Jesus leave us a book and tell us to figure it out individually–or did He establish a Church and entrust it with the authority to teach, preserve, and interpret what He revealed?"

That night was when the lights turned on for me. I realized our debates always collapsed for the same reason: we were starting in the middle of the story, arguing interpretations without first settling authority. Out of that conversation came the simple, steady approach I use in this book:

1. Establish common ground. First confirm what nearly all Christians should affirm: God sent Jesus; Jesus taught and commissioned His apostles; and the apostles preached, taught, and governed the Church. If we can't stand together here, nothing else will stand.

2. Ask, do not attack. "Who says or where did you learn that X is wrong?" Make the source explicit. Is it a pastor? A website? A chain of private interpretations? This slows the conversation down and exposes assumptions without shaming the person.

3. Return to origins and authority. "How did we get the Bible?" Who recognized its books? Who has Christ-given authority to decide disputed meanings? Once you see that the canon and teaching office arise from the apostolic Church, verse-dueling gives way to the larger, logical picture Christ Himself designed.

4. Don't look to win, look to be prepared to give a defense for the faith that has been given.

I still pray "Come, Holy Spirit" before hard conversations. I still try to answer objections clearly. But that night taught me something better than winning a point: begin with unity in first truths, ask clarifying questions, and then take people back to the Church Jesus founded—the only setting where Scripture, tradition, and authority make sense together. Sometimes all you can do is plant a seed. Often, that's exactly what the Holy Spirit will use.

CONCLUSION

Stand in What You Have Received

God sent Jesus; Jesus commissioned the Apostles; the Apostles preached, wrote, and appointed successors, building up a visible Church; and Christ promised the Holy Spirit would guide her to the end.

- God sent Jesus.

- Jesus commissioned the Apostles.

- The Apostles preached, wrote, and appointed successors.

- Thus, a visible Church was built.

- Christ promised the Holy Spirit to guide her to the end.

The next time anyone says, *"Catholics are wrong,"* there is no reason to be on the defensive. You do not need to be a scholar to understand Christ and His Church—you need a childlike heart. That is different from being childish. Paul tells us to put away childish things (1 Cor 13:11), while Jesus says we must *become like children* to enter the kingdom (Mt 18:3). Childishness refuses to learn; childlikeness trusts and receives.

That is how the Church began to make sense to me. As a child, I knew my parents loved me without a dissertation. I knew it in simple signs—French toast, spaghetti and meatballs, a hand teaching me to cast a line. I did not analyze the love; I received it. So it is with God. In and through the Church, love is given, not solved—Jesus's own Body and Blood offered to us. We can study the mystery (and should), but we do not have to master it to receive it. Come with a child's trust: what the Church hands on, Christ Himself hands to you.

You do not need to be fearful, intimidated, or embarrassed when you hear "Catholics are wrong." You only need to stand where Christ stands with the Church He founded, the Apostles He sent, and the Spirit He promised, and ask, *"Says who?"* All through this book, we have kept the same rhythm:

- **Agreements:** God sent Jesus; Jesus taught and commissioned; the Apostles preached and taught.

- **Ask:** "Why do you think that?" "Who/where did you learn that X is wrong?" "Are you sure that is true?"

- **Authority:** Canon fact and Christ's structure; the same Church that recognized the Bible is the Church that preserves its true meaning.

This is not a clever debate trick; it's simple reason and logic. If God revealed Himself in Christ, then His teaching needed a reliable way to be preserved, recognized, and applied across time. A universal community requires a public authority to settle disputes, or else it fragments into competing claims. The existence of a visible body with ordered leadership is therefore not an add-on but the rational consequence of revelation: truth given for all must be guarded for all.

Clement of Rome (c. A.D. 96) was a disciple of Peter. He writes that the apostles **appointed bishops and deacons** and provided for successors when they died—explicit apostolic succession.

Ignatius of Antioch (c. A.D. 107), a Disciple of John, insists Christians must remain united to their **bishop**, because where the bishop is, there is the Church. He also uses the term "Catholic" to describe the Church.

So the Church answers errors not with outrage, but with clarity (because truth is knowable), charity (because people matter), and confidence (because promises bind). In short, unity, authority, and continuity aren't arbitrary—they are what sound reason says that any enduring, worldwide teaching mission must have.

The phrase *"All I need is the Bible"* sounds humble. It sounds like submission. But it often functions as the opposite: **a denial of authority while quietly installing the self as the final authority**. Human beings cannot live without a hierarchy of judgment. If you remove a legitimate, public authority, something else immediately fills the vacuum— usually the individual ego, and often unconsciously. Here is the circular structure:

- *I trust the Bible because it is the Word of God.*

- *I know which books are the Word of God because they are in the Bible.*

But the Bible does not list its own contents. It does not hand you a divinely inspired table of contents. The canon is received—handed down— and recognized within the life of the Church. So, the claim "Bible alone" rests on an assumption it cannot justify from within itself. It borrows the Church's conclusion (the canon) while denying the Church's authority to make it.

This is why debates quickly devolve into endless stalemates. Because once the Church is removed as a living court, there is no common court left. The individual becomes the judge of everything:

- Which books belong in Scripture
- What a passage "really" means
- What doctrines are essential
- Who is saved and who is not

And now the burden is placed where no human being can carry it without distortion: on private interpretation as the final court of appeal. In practice, this produces not unity but fragmentation— competing claims, multiplying denominations, and a constant pressure to protect identity. When interpretation is personal sovereignty, disagreement feels like betrayal. The truth must be defended not only as a proposition, but as a fragile self-definition.

That is why the Catholic claim is not an "add-on." It is the rational consequence of revelation. If God revealed Himself in Christ for the whole world, then that revelation required a reliable way to be preserved, recognized, and applied across time— publicly, consistently, and authoritatively. A universal message requires a universal household. A constitution without a court yields endless lawsuits; likewise, a Bible without a living, authorized teacher yields endless interpretations.

So, the question beneath "Catholics are wrong" is never merely *Which verse?* It is always: **Who gets to say what the verse finally means?** And that question does not go away. It only hides behind slogans.

If we're honest, most people don't leave the Church because they've carefully studied doctrine and concluded it's false; they leave because they don't like **authority**—especially when that authority makes real claims on their behavior. This is human nature, and it's particularly visible in adolescence: testing limits, resisting guidance, wanting the bene- fits of belonging without the burdens of obedi- ence. In practice, the drift is rarely from "Catholic to a better-argued theology," but from Catholic to no religion at all, or to a version of Christianity that demands less— "I'm born again; me and my Bible are enough; I'm saved"—where the individual becomes the final referee.

The Catholic Church, by contrast, is not shy about moral authority because it believes Christ actu- ally entrusted it to her. She teaches chastity (no sex outside marriage), opposes contraception as contrary to the meaning of marital love, binds the faithful to Mass on Sundays and holy days of obliga- tion, calls us to confession when we fall, and asks for fasting and almsgiving as concrete expressions of repentance and love.

None of this flatters our pride or indulges our comfort, which is exactly why it's easy to resent—and exactly why it forms saints. Authority feels abrasive when we want autonomy; it feels liberating when we want the **truth** that can shape a life. The myth is "people leave because of doctrine"; the reality, nine times out of ten, is "people leave because doctrine comes with a **yoke**." The Church does not apologize for that yoke; she simply repeats her Master: *take it up and find rest for your souls*.

In the end, each person has the choice. God gives us freedom to believe and to follow Christ—or not. Following Him is often hard; we won't always understand or agree with everything He teaches. But discipleship means taking up the cross (Mt 16:24) and trusting His guidance more than our preferences.

In Scripture, Paul warns the sailors, "Except these abide in the ship, ye cannot be saved" (Acts 27:31). That's a fitting image for the Church: stay in the boat Christ founded, rather than claiming belief while inventing private interpretations (see 2 Pt 1:20, 3:16). We can either remain within the household God established—trusting His promises—or drift into a sea of opinions that cannot save.

As you go forward, aim for three things:

1. **Clarity without combat:** decline verse duels. Keep returning to Jesus → Apostles → Church.

2. **Confidence without pride:** it is Christ's Church, not your personal project. Let Him carry the weight.

3. **Charity without compromise:** honor the good you see (including a real personal love for Jesus) while inviting friends into the fullness Christ intends—Scripture within the Church, sacramental life, and unity under the shepherds He gave us.

A Simple Rule of Life

- **Pray daily, especially the rosary** (15-20 minutes). Name the people you hope to help.

- **Stay sacramental** (Sunday Mass, regular Confession).

- **Follow the readings each Sunday.** You will have read most of the Bible in three years of Sunday Mass.

- **Keep learning** (a page of the Creed/Catechism each week; one short source per topic).

- **Practice the script** with a friend until it is second nature.

Quick Send-Off

When someone says, *"Catholics are wrong,"* I first highlight what we share, ask where the claim originates, recall how we received the Bible, and then examine how Jesus actually established things—through the Apostles and the Church—so we can follow Him together.

A Short Prayer

Lord Jesus, you built Your Church and promised the Spirit of truth. Make me steady, kind, and clear. Let my words honor Your Word, my life honor Your Body, and my love draw others home. Amen.

Remember, you are not alone in this. The same Lord who breathed on the Apostles breathes courage into you. Step forward with peace. The truth is beautiful—and it belongs to every seeker you meet.

Changing Minds

Always be respectful and keep in mind that people rarely change their views on the spot. In all the many conversations I have had over the years, only one person saw the logic and began his journey back to the Church immediately following our conversation. Pure logic alone will seldom result in immediate change. People often need time to think and reflect.

Nevertheless, it is a starting point. It will also help your interlocutor discover that when they say "Catholics are wrong," the answer to "Says who?" is ultimately their individual interpretation and belief. The best you can hope for is to plant a seed and let God do the rest.

There are many reasons that people have difficulty changing their minds. Think about how hard it might have been for you to have changed your belief about something in the past. Here are some common reasons why people find it difficult to understand. These might be helpful to keep in mind when dialoguing with others.

Cognitive and psychological:

- **Identity protection:** "If I admit this, who am I now?" Beliefs are tied to family, mentors, and self-story.

- **Sunk cost and commitment bias:** years of preaching/teaching a view make reversal feel impossible.

- **Confirmation and availability bias:** their sources, sermons, and feeds keep supplying the same answers.

- **Loss aversion:** the *costs* of changing (community, vocation, reputation) feel larger than the *benefits*.

- **Affect heuristic:** "Catholicism makes me feel uneasy." → "Therefore, it must be wrong."

Social and relational:

- **Community ties:** Church = friends, spouse, job, identity. Conversion risks loneliness or conflict at home.

- **Trusted authorities:** a beloved pastor said X; loyalty competes with evidence.

- **Group boundaries:** "We are not like them" can be a powerful, unspoken rule.

Paradigm differences:

- *Sola Scriptura* **lens:** if "Bible alone + my/ our reading" is the starting rule, appeals to Tradition, councils, or the Church will feel like category errors.

- **Perspicuity assumption:** "The Bible is clear on essentials" makes Catholic distinctives look like add-ons.

- **Authority allergy:** "No living authority can bind me" is a prior commitment that blocks the Catholic conclusion regardless of data.

Historical and moral stumbling blocks:

- **Scandals and sins:** past or recent failures are taken as disproof of Catholic claims.

- **History taught selectively:** textbook or pulpit narratives (e.g., "Rome invented X in the Middle Ages") feel definitive.

- **Misunderstandings:** Mary/saints = idolatry; Eucharist = "re-sacrifice"; papacy = mere power. If those frames stay intact, logic will not land.

Practical barriers:

- **Overwhelming:** the learning curve (Creed, councils, Fathers) feels too steep.

- **Time/attention scarcity:** life is busy; re-examining foundations is costly.

- **Fear of being deceived:** "If I change once, what stops me from changing again?"

Spiritual dynamics:

- **Habituated prayer/worship style:** we attach to how we meet God.

- **Moral stakes:** some fear that Catholic moral teaching will require hard changes.

- **Grace and timing:** conversion is also God's work; insight often arrives gradually.

How to respond (brief playbook):

- **Lead with common ground:** reaffirm Christ, Scripture, grace. (It lowers defenses.)

- **Ask, do not pounce:** "What would *count* as good evidence for you?" "What would you need to see?"

- **Name the paradigm gently:** "If Scripture must be self-interpreting, any appeal to history will sound wrong—can we examine that starting rule together?"

- **Use lived continuity:** Creed → canon → council → worship (Acts 2:42; Acts 15) as a single throughline, not scattered proofs.

- **Differentiate scandals from doctrine:** "Failure violates Catholic teaching; it doesn't define it."

- **Offer low-friction steps:** read one Father (Ignatius, Irenaeus), one council text, attend one Mass, pray one week with John 6.

- **Be patient and pray:** you can win an argument and lose a soul. Aim for clarity and charity.

What Protestants Would Say

What I have attempted to demonstrate is a conceptualization of the Church that Christ established over two thousand years ago and a basic response grounded in logic and reasoning to assertions that "Catholics are wrong." While it would be impossible in these pages to present every Protestant claim and challenge, here are two of the most common—stated fairly in their own best terms—followed by a concise Catholic reply.

Apostolic Succession Doesn't Guarantee Apostolic Truth

The Protestant claim (fairly stated):

What ultimately matters is fidelity to the Apostles' doctrine, not an unbroken line of hands. A tactile lineage can pass on error just as easily as truth (see Paul correcting Peter in Gal 2:11-14). Scripture is the norm that norms (2 Tm 3:16-17), and a Church is "apostolic" when it preaches the Gospel purely and administers the sacraments rightly (Acts 17:11; Gal 1:8). Succession without doctrinal fidelity is empty.

Catholic reply:

Catholics say "both/and," not either/or. The New Testament shows doctrine and office together: the faith is handed on "to faithful men, who shall be able

to teach others also" (2 Tm 2:2), by public ordina-
tion/laying on of hands (Acts 6:6, 14:23; 1 Tm 4:14;
2 Tm 1:6). The Church is a visible household that
can actually judge disputes—"tell it unto the church"
(Mt 18:17)—and is called "the pillar and ground of
the truth" (1 Tm 3:15). Apostolic succession doesn't
replace fidelity; it is the ordinary means by which
fidelity is guarded and recognized for the whole
flock. Without a living, accountable office, "apostolic truth" collapses into competing private claims—
good preaching, yes, but no public arbiter when
preachers disagree.

The "Gates of Hell" Promise

The Protestant claim (fairly stated):

When Jesus says, "the gates of hell shall not
prevail" (Mt 16:18), Protestants claim that Christ
promises the perseverance of the Gospel and His
people, not the indefectibility of one institution. The
true Church is the body of believers across time and
space. Even if Rome erred, the promise stands—
God always preserves a faithful people. Therefore,
the verse does not entail the Catholic claims about
papal primacy or a singular visible communion.

Catholic reply:

Catholics agree the promise is about the perseverance of Christ's work—and the New Testament

depicts that work as a visible Church with real authority: Peter receives the keys and the power to bind and loose (Mt 16:19), is charged to strengthen the brethren (Lk 22:32), and feed Christ's sheep (Jn 21:15-17).

Moreover, the Apostles establish leaders by laying on of hands (Acts 14:23), and when controversy erupts, the Church renders a public, binding judgment (Acts 15, 16:4). The "gates of hell" fits this picture: Christ safeguards a recognizable body that can actually teach, decide, and endure—not just scattered individuals who happen to agree. The Gospel that endures is the Gospel as preached, celebrated, and guarded in the Church that Christ founded.

Why these two claims matter in dialogue:

Both claims redirect the debate to authority. If "apostolic" reduces to "my/our reading of Scripture," then there is no common court when sincere Christians disagree (2 Pt 3:16). Catholicism proposes that Christ provided one: a teaching Church with apostolic succession and a Petrine center to serve unity—so that the same Gospel is preached, the same Eucharist is celebrated, and the same rule of faith is publicly identifiable across ages and nations (Mt 18:17; 1 Tm 3:15; Jn 16:13).

The Heart of Authority

Scripture's own pattern shows the Apostles handing on a *living office*, not just handing out books.

- They ordain by laying on of hands: the Seven (Acts 6:6), Paul and Barnabas (Acts 13:3), presbyters in every church (Acts 14:23).

- Timothy receives a gift through laying on of hands (1 Tm 4:14; 2 Tm 1:6) and is told to guard the deposit (1 Tm 6:20; 2 Tm 1:13-14).

- Titus is left in Crete to appoint elders in each city (Ti 1:5).

- Doctrine is transmitted person-to-person with the expectation of *further* transmission: "the things that thou hast heard of me … commit thou to faithful men, who shall be able to teach others also" (2 Tm 2:2).

- And the churches are commanded to hold the traditions delivered "by word, or our epistle" (2 Thes 2:15).

If the plan were "Bible alone," none of that makes much sense. The New Testament was not yet compiled; yet the Apostles govern, teach, ordain, correct, and decide disputes (see Acts 15) through a visible structure that can bind consciences.

The laying on of hands is the concrete sign that ministry is not self-appointed and doctrine is not a private possession; it is received and entrusted within the Church so that the same Gospel is preserved intact across time and place.

A simple way to see it: the Bible is the constitution; the apostolic ministry is the living court and legislature that reads it rightly, applies it, and hands on the rule of faith. A constitution without any court yields endless fragmentation; likewise, a Bible without a living, authorized ministry yields endless, unresolvable interpretations.

So what are we to make of the Apostles training successors and imposing hands? Exactly what the text shows: Christ intended a Church with continuing, public shepherds—a succession that safeguards Scripture, settles controversy, and feeds the flock—so that the people of God would not be "tossed to and fro by every wind of doctrine" (Eph 4:14).

To say then that the Church fell away—whether in Mormon terms ("Great Apostasy") or in the practical Protestant storyline ("the Church drifted so far that it had to be recovered")—is to imply that the Apostles' work was ineffective and Christ's public promises failed. If the Church truly collapsed, then these promises either never meant what they say or were defective in effect—an unthinkable conclusion. The

Catholic claim is simpler and more faithful to the text: the Church can be wounded by sinners and in need of reform, yet never defect from the apostolic faith.

That is why, across centuries and cultures, one visible communion still teaches one Creed, celebrates one Eucharist, and maintains one apostolic line—not because her members are flawless, but because Christ keeps His word.

Test Case

Here is the uncomfortable but clarifying fact-pattern: if Christ really promised that His Church would be guided into all truth and that "the gates of hell shall not prevail," then we should expect her not to err in faith and morals when the culture shifts—and contraception is a case in point. For nearly two millennia, all major Christian bodies taught that intentionally rendering the marital act sterile is morally wrong; the first major break came in 1930, when the Anglican bishops at the Lambeth Conference (Resolution 15) cautiously permitted artificial means in limited cases, reversing their own prior condemnations.

Within a generation, most Protestant denominations followed that lead. The Catholic Church, by contrast, explicitly reaffirmed the perennial teaching the very same year in Pius XI's *Casti Connubii* (1930), and again—prophetically—in Paul VI's *Humanae Vitae* (1968), which warned of the social and political harms that would follow normalization of contraception.

Pastoral reality is what it is—many Catholics ignore the teaching—but the Church's doctrine has not changed, precisely because she believes she cannot reverse a moral norm taught by Scripture, Tradition, and the ordinary and universal Magisterium.

In other words, when a storm hit, one communion shifted with the winds; the other stood on the promise that Christ would preserve His Church's moral witness. That improbable steadiness over time—teaching one rule where others yielded—is exactly the kind of sign you'd expect if Christ really keeps His word.

Some Common Objections

What I've offered in this book is a basic defense that politely turns the tables by asking, "Says who"? Before we duel with verses, we ask the prior questions: How did we get the Bible? Who decides between competing interpretations? Did Jesus leave a living authority or not? This isn't because Scripture is weak; it's because private interpretation is endless. Two sincere Christians can quote the same Bible and still disagree forever.

With that groundwork in place, we can now turn to some common objections to Catholic teaching. Many Catholics hear these questions—sometimes from friends, family members, or online debates—and aren't always sure how to respond. Most objections sound persuasive because they are framed as simple biblical claims, but when we slow down and ask the deeper questions, we've been asking all along—how Scripture came to us, who has the authority to interpret it, and how the early Church handled real disagreements—the force of these challenges often fades.

What follows is not about winning arguments, but about understanding the Catholic faith more clearly and being able to explain it with confidence, clarity, and charity. With that aim in mind, I've outlined seven of the most common objections Catholics encounter, provided a reference table of frequently cited Bible verses, and offered a clearer explanation of how the Bible itself came to be. For readers who wish to go further, I've also included additional resources to help deepen understanding beyond this section.

The Eucharist Is Only a Symbol?: Look at Worship

Avoid debates over interpretation and observe how Christians actually worshiped in the earliest communities. Instead of focusing on arguments over words, consider the evidence found in the actual practices of the first believers: they gathered to break bread, prayed together, and treated the Eucharist with profound reverence that went beyond mere symbolism.

On the night of the Last Supper, Jesus took the cup and said, "This cup is the New Testament in my blood ... this do in remembrance of me" (Lk 22:19-

20; see 1 Cor 11:24-25 KJV). Not *write*, but *do this* in remembrance of me.

In Scripture, "testament" means "covenant" (Greek *diathēkē*). So before the "New Testament" was a book, it was a sacrament—a covenantal act by which Christ sealed the new and eternal covenant in His Blood and commanded the Church to do it.

As former Protestant and theologian Dr. Scott Hahn loves to say, *before the New Testament was a document, it was a sacrament*. The Eucharist is thus not a mere memorial; it is the covenant meal of the New Testament people, the place where the written Word is proclaimed and the incarnate Word gives us His Body and Blood in fulfillment of His promise.

Their actions—uniting around the table, speaking of participation in the Body and Blood of Christ, and passing down these traditions—demonstrate a lived understanding that the Eucharist is real and sacred, not merely a memory or representation.

This concrete expression of faith reveals that, for the earliest Christians, the Eucharist was an encounter with Christ's actual presence, nourishing both the individual and the community in ways far deeper than a symbolic gesture.

Historical testimonies, such as those from Ignatius of Antioch and Justin Martyr, consistently describe the Eucharist as more than a symbolic act—they affirm a real presence and transformative encounter. The continuity of these practices, maintained across diverse regions, points to a shared conviction rooted in the apostolic tradition, rather than later invention or mere metaphor.

From the start, Christians gathered on the first day of the week for "the breaking of bread," and the Apostles' teaching (Acts 2:42, 20:7). Roman authorities viewed this new movement with suspicion because Christians would not sacrifice to the emperor or pagan gods. Despite stigma, legal risk, and waves of persecution, Christians kept meeting every Sunday to "break bread." They did not treat it as a symbol they could postpone; they risked their lives to receive it. That stubborn fact—attested by pagans and Christians alike—strongly supports what the Church has always believed about the real, vital importance of the Eucharist in the life of the early Church.

This same approach—looking to lived worship rather than abstract interpretation—helps to clarify what early Christians believed. The genuine faith of the ancient Church is often better seen in its prayers, rituals, and actions than in later theological debates.

When we witness their devotion and practices, we find continuity with what the Church still professes today: that the Eucharist is an encounter with Christ Himself, not a mere symbol.

Confession to a Priest?

Early practice to observe:

Christians confessed grave sins to the Church's ministers, received penance and reconciliation, and returned to full communion. This was never about replacing God; it was about receiving His forgiveness through the means He established. "Again, Jesus said, 'Peace be with you! As the Father has sent me, I am sending you.' And with that, he breathed on them and said,

> *'Receive the Holy Spirit. If you forgive anyone's sins, their sins are forgiven; if you do not forgive them, they are not forgiven" (Jn 20:21-23).*

The Lord wants us to come to Him when we fall—often, and with confidence. He also made mercy tangible by breathing the Holy Spirit on the Apostles and entrusting them with absolute authority to bind and loose, to reconcile sinners to God and the community. In the Church, Christ extends His merciful presence across generations. In the words of Paul, "All this is from God, who through

Christ reconciled us to himself and gave us the ministry of reconciliation" (2 Cor 5:18).

The Apostles and their successors are merely ambassadors for Christ (2 Cor 5:20), bringing his forgiveness to the world through the sacraments and the gospel. If God has chosen to bring his message of forgiveness to the world by means of sinful, human ambassadors, why would he not be able to give these messengers the power to forgive and retain sins? Moreover, why would this not be a natural way for Jesus to extend his merciful presence on earth for all generations?

Papal Infallibility?

Foundation and continuity:

After asking the disciples who men say he is, it is Peter who replies, "You are the Christ, the Son of the living God" (Mt 16:16). Christ then says to Peter, "Blessed are you, Simon Bar-Jonah, for flesh and blood has not revealed *this* to you, but My Father who is in heaven. And I also say to you that you are Peter, and on this rock I will build My church, and the gates of Hades shall not prevail against it. And I will give you the keys of the kingdom of heaven, and whatever you bind on earth will be bound in heaven, and whatever you loose on earth will be loosed in heaven" (Mt 16:17–19).

When Jesus tells Peter, "I will give unto thee the keys of the kingdom of heaven …" (Mt 16:19), he echoes the Davidic "key" imagery of Isaiah 22:22, where the king's chief steward receives "the key of the house of David" with authority to open, and none shall shut, and shut and none shall open.

In the Davidic kingdom, the key signified delegated royal authority—the steward governed the household in the king's name. Christ, the Son of David, is the true King (see Rv 3:7), and by giving Peter the keys—together with the power to bind and loose—He establishes Peter as the visible steward of His Church, a primacy of service ordered to safeguarding unity and doctrine in the royal household of God.

The household of God is "built upon the foundation of the apostles" (Eph 2:20). From the beginning, unity and teaching were served by connected leadership—locally by bishops, and in universal communion through Peter's service to unity.

Jesus did not say, "Upon this book I will build." He said, "Upon this rock"—addressing Peter, to whom He entrusted not only the keys and a singular role of strengthening the brethren, but also the power to bind and lose. The Church is not founded on paper but on the apostolic foundation that Christ Himself appointed.

Imagine a huge hospital. The chief surgeon (the "king") runs it, but he also appoints a chief of staff and gives her a master keycard. That keycard doesn't make her the owner; it lets her open what others can't, lock what must be locked, and coordinate the whole house when decisions are needed.

That's the sense of the Davidic key (Is 22) and Jesus giving Peter the keys (Mt 16:19). Christ is the true Head; Peter receives the steward's master key—authority delegated for **service**—so the household (the Church) can stay united, doors can be opened or shut wisely ("bind and loose"), and patient care (our salvation) isn't left to chaos.

Examine how leadership and unity actually functioned across churches and how servant leadership preserved communion. According to Scripture, Christ founded a visible Church that would never cease to exist and had the authority to teach and discipline believers (see Mt 16:18-19, 18:17).

St. Paul tells us that this Church is "the pillar and foundation of truth" (1 Tm 3:15) and it was built on "the foundation of the apostles" (Eph 2:20). Paul also tells us the Church would have a hierarchy composed of deacons (1 Tm 2:8-13); presbyters, from where we get the English word *priest* (1 Tm 5:17); and bishops (1 Tm 3:1-7).

Paul even instructed one of these bishops, Titus, to appoint priests on the island of Crete (Ti 1:5). In 110 CE, St. Ignatius of Antioch told his readers, "Follow the bishop, even as Jesus Christ does the Father, and the presbytery as you would the apostles; and reverence the deacons, as being the institution of God. Let no man do anything connected with the Church without the bishop."

What Infallibility Is

- **A safety net against error:** it is an exceptional help of the Holy Spirit that prevents the Church (and in some instances, the pope) from teaching error when defining a doctrine of faith or morals.

- **For the whole Church:** it is used when the pope intends to bind all Catholics on a matter of faith/morals to be held definitively (this is called speaking *ex cathedra*), or when the bishops together with the pope teach something as to be held definitively (e.g., an ecumenical council), or when the world's bishops, in union with the pope, consistently and definitively teach the same doctrine (the ordinary and universal Magisterium).

- **About preserving the deposit of faith:** it does not invent new truths; it guards and clarifies what Christ handed down through Scripture and Tradition.

- **Rare and careful:** Explicit papal *ex cathedra* definitions are rare (classic examples: Immaculate Conception in 1854, Assumption of Mary in 1950).

What Infallibility Is Not

- **Not inspiration:** the pope is not "dictating Scripture." He is protected from error in a defined act; he is not receiving a new revelation.

- **Not impeccability (sinlessness):** it says nothing about personal holiness. A pope can sin, make bad administrative calls, or be imprudent.

- **Not every word or interview:** homilies, opinions, off-the-cuff remarks, prudential policies, disciplinary rules, and even many encyclical passages are not automatically infallible. They can be authoritative and deserve respect, but they are not immune to error unless they clearly meet the conditions above.

- **Not a new doctrine:** an infallible definition does not invent a belief; it confirms what belongs to the faith (sometimes after long reflection or controversy).

The Basic Checklist

1. The pope acts as universal shepherd (not as private theologian or local bishop).

2. He speaks on faith or morals.

3. He intends to define—to settle the question definitively.

4. He intends to bind the whole Church.

If all four are present, the teaching is **infallible**.

Other Ways the Church Teaches Infallibly

- Ecumenical councils, with the pope, define doctrines for the whole Church (e.g., Nicaea, Trent, Vatican II—when they clearly intend to define matters of faith/morals).

- The ordinary and universal Magisterium: when bishops worldwide, in union with the pope, consistently and definitively teach the same doctrine as belonging to the faith (even without a single "defining moment").

What Catholics Owe to Church Teaching

- **To infallible teachings:** complete, irrevocable assent (because they are guaranteed to be accurate).

- **To non-infallible but authoritative teachings:** a real, "religious submission of mind and will" (a presumption of truth and willingness to be taught), while recognizing they are not proposed as definitive.

One-minute takeaway

Infallibility is God's gift of protection, not a power to invent ideas. It prevents error when the Church— or the pope, in particular conditions—definitively teaches a doctrine of faith or morals for the whole Church. It is rare, carefully used, and always aimed at handing on (not changing) what Christ gave the Apostles.

Development vs. "New Ideas"

The Church does not invent new doctrines; she sometimes comes to understand more deeply what God revealed once for all in Christ (see Jude 1:3). Think of an acorn becoming an oak: the identity is the same, but its meaning and implications unfold over time. Classic examples include the Trinity and the two natures of Christ—truths believed for centuries, later expressed with greater clarity and precision.

How to tell authentic development from novelty:

- **Continuity of identity:** the later teaching says the same thing in a fuller way (deeper precision), not something different that contradicts what came before.

- **Organic growth, not rupture:** language may sharpen (e.g., "consubstantial"), practices may mature, but the substance of the faith remains intact.

- **Rooted in the same sources:** genuine development springs from Scripture read in the Church, apostolic Tradition, and continuous worship/prayer—not from passing opinion or cultural pressure.

- **Received by the Church:** over time, the whole Church recognizes and lives the development—the law of prayer shapes the law of belief.

Why infallibility matters here:

When controversy arises, the Church's infallible judgments do not create new revelations; they fix the boundaries of what the deposit of faith already contains—often using more precise language to exclude errors and to protect the truth for future generations. These are not new ideas, but a deeper grasp of the same revelation—development without alteration.

Mary and the Saints: Honor vs. Worship

Without Mary, there is no Christ—not because God needed her in an absolute sense, but because God freely chose to come to us through her. In the economy of salvation, Mary is the Theotokos (Mother of God): by her fiat—"Let it be done to me according to your word" (Lk 1:38)—the eternal Son truly takes on flesh. Her "yes" is the human doorway through which the Incarnation enters history.

In this sense, Mary is the Church's first disciple and, analogically, the first Apostle—not one of the Twelve, but the first to receive, bear, and bring Christ to others. She believes before she understands (see Lk 2:19, 2:51), carries the Word-made-flesh to Elizabeth (the Visitation), sings the Magnificat, presents Him in the Temple, and stands at the Cross (Jn 19:25-27). After the Resurrection, she is found praying with the Apostles as they await Pentecost (Acts 1:14). Her path is the template of Christian life: hear the word, say yes, carry Christ, stand firm in suffering, pray with the Church, and receive the Spirit.

Calling her the "first Apostle" is a way to highlight this missionary pattern: she receives Christ, bears Him to the world, and points to Him ("Do whatever He tells you," Jn 2:5). She is never a rival to Christ's unique mediation nor to the apostolic office He gave the Twelve; instead, she is the model of how to receive and hand on Christ.

Honor here never replaces worship of God; it is love for what God loves. "All generations will call me blessed" (Lk 1:48). Honoring the mother of the Lord is a Christ-centered instinct: it magnifies what God has done in her and invites us to imitate her faith, humility, and obedience. Even key Protestant reformers spoke reverently of Mary in ways many forget today. Here is what Martin Luther said of Mary:

> "The true honor of Mary is the honor of God, the praise of God's grace. God has given Mary the honor to be the Mother of God, and this honor we all wish to give her, to praise her highly, and to hold her in respect." (*Explanation of the Magnificat*, 1521)

> "[She is the] highest woman and the noblest gem in Christianity after Christ … We can never honor her enough. Still honor and praise must be given to her in such a way as to injure neither Christ nor the Scriptures." (Christmas Sermon, 1531)

Observe the Church's lived distinction between worship of God and honor for His friends. This distinction is evident in Christian practice, where veneration of saints—especially Mary—reflects a deep respect for those who have faithfully followed Christ, yet always preserves the unique adoration owed to God alone. The Church's liturgy, prayers, and artistic expressions consistently direct worship toward God, while acts such as asking saints for intercession or celebrating their feast days serve to honor their exemplary lives and encourage believers to imitate their virtues.

This balanced approach safeguards the primacy of divine worship. It underscores the communion of saints as a testament to God's transformative grace in the lives of His people, setting the stage for the Church's reverent use of sacred images, which further instruct and inspire the faithful without diminishing the glory reserved for God.

Images and Idolatry: What Christians Actually Did

What God forbids—and what He commanded:

Idolatry is forbidden; adoration is due to God alone. However, in the Old Covenant, God also commanded specific sacred images (the cherubim over the Ark; the bronze serpent as a sign of healing). Early Christians used sacred art as teaching and memory aids while firmly reserving adoration for God. In this way, the Church's reverent use of images never confuses honor with worship, and the faithful are continually reminded that the veneration shown to sacred art points beyond itself to the reality of God's grace and the lives transformed by Him. The distinction between adoration and veneration is safeguarded not only by doctrine but also by the lived experience of Christian communities, where images serve as visual catechesis—inviting believers to reflect on the mysteries of faith, imitate the holiness of saints, and deepen their devotion to Christ—while always upholding the primacy of worship owed to God alone.

When you look at a photo of someone you love, you are not loving the paper—you are loving the person it represents. The image mediates memory and affection; it helps your heart turn toward the one you love. That is the logic behind holy images: they are reminders, not replacements. In Catholic terms, worship (*latria*) belongs to God alone; honor (*dulia*) given to saints—and *hyperdulia* uniquely to Mary—directs our love toward God's friends. Because of the Incarnation (God made visible in Christ), using visible signs to lift our minds to invisible realities is not idolatry but good pedagogy for the heart.

Salvation: Grace, Faith, and the Life That Follows

Look how the earliest Church formed disciples: grace received in faith, lived in conversion, worship, and love. In this unfolding journey, salvation is not a one-time event, but a dynamic process that draws believers ever deeper into the life of Christ and the community He established. The Church, from its earliest days, has invited each person to ongoing transformation—encountering God's mercy in the sacraments, persevering in prayer and in acts of charity, and participating in communal worship that shapes identity and mission.

Thus, salvation is experienced as both a gift to be received and a calling to be lived out, drawing the faithful into the communion of the Church and preparing them for the fullness of life with God—a reality that bridges the apostolic age and the continuing witness of the Church today. Jesus's command to "come after Me" by taking up our cross (see Mt 16:24; Mk 8:34; Lk 9:23) underscores the call to active discipleship rather than mere intellectual belief. He invites followers not only to assent to His teachings but also to embrace a life marked by self-denial, perseverance, and sacrificial love. This command reveals that authentic faith is inseparable from action: it requires us to follow Christ on the path of daily conversion, willingly accepting trials, and surrendering our own desires to God's will.

In the context of the Church's understanding of salvation, this teaching aligns with the journey of grace received and faith lived. Picking up our cross means engaging in a dynamic process of transformation—participating in worship, acts of charity, and ongoing conversion—so that belief is expressed through a life shaped by Christ's example. Thus, Jesus's call moves believers beyond passive acceptance toward a committed response, making discipleship a living testimony to God's love and mercy in the world.

Traditions of Men

Many of our friends—especially in some Protestant circles—see Jesus criticize the Pharisees and conclude that all tradition is bad. However, in the Gospels, Jesus condemns "traditions of men" that nullify God's command (Mk 7:8, 7:13), not the very idea of tradition. In fact, the New Testament speaks of tradition positively. St. Paul instructs his readers to "Stand firm and hold to the traditions you were taught by word or by letter" (2 Thes 2:15), and "I commend you because you maintain the traditions" (1 Cor 11:2). The issue is not tradition vs. no tradition; it is human, manmade additions that contradict God's word vs. the apostolic Tradition that faithfully hands on Christ's teaching.

Why We Need Apostolic Tradition

How do we *have* the biblical texts?

- The Apostles and their coworkers wrote to real churches; those churches copied, preserved, and circulated the writings in worship.

- Bishops and deacons oversaw archives and readings; monks later hand-copied manuscripts for centuries.

- Without the Church's custody (liturgy, libraries, copyists), much of Scripture would have vanished.

How do we know the Bible is *trustworthy*?

- The same communities that received the Apostles publicly read these texts, compared them with the "rule of faith" (Creed-shaped summary), and rejected counterfeits.

- Trust rests on a living chain of witnesses (bishops in succession) who preserved authentic texts and corrected corrupt ones.

How do we know which books belong in Scripture? (the canon)

- The Bible does not list its own table of contents.

- Local usage converged and was recognized by the Church (e.g., Rome 382; Hippo 393; Carthage 397/419), producing the same New Testament we use today, and the Catholic Old Testament received from early Christian practice.

- This is recognition, not invention—an act of the Church's discernment, not private opinion.

How are they to be *interpreted*?

- From the start, Scripture was read in the Church's worship, under pastors in apostolic succession, using the rule of faith as the guardrail (e.g., Trinity, Incarnation).

- When disputes arose, councils clarified the meaning in line with the Apostles (e.g., Nicaea on Christ's divinity).

- The Magisterium serves Scripture by giving authoritative (not arbitrary) judgments, so the one Gospel is preserved across time and cultures.

Snapshot summary:

- **Texts:** safeguarded by the Church's life.

- **Trustworthiness:** verified in a living community with a rule of faith.

- **Canon:** recognized by the Church, so all share the same Scriptures.

- **Interpretation:** guided by apostolic teaching, councils, and worship.

Scripture and apostolic Tradition are not rivals. Scripture is God's written Word; apostolic Tradition is the living transmission of that Word in the Church Christ founded—so Christians can know what the Word is and what it means.

Examples of Protestant Reliance on Tradition

- **The canon itself:** the Bible's table of contents is a received tradition; Scripture does not list its own books.

- **Chapter and verse numbers:** medieval and sixteenth-century additions that are useful, but not in the original texts.

- **Sunday worship:** the Lord's Day custom comes from the early Church's practice, not an explicit command to abandon the Sabbath.

- **Nicene Christianity:** most Protestants accept the Trinity and Nicene Creed—definitions forged by councils (Tradition interpreting Scripture).

- **Worship formats:** sermon-centric services, congregational singing, altar calls, the

"sinner's prayer," midweek Bible study—
traditions developed over time.

- **Doctrinal slogans:** even *Sola Scriptura* is a
post-biblical tradition about how to read the
Bible.

- **Moral/disciplinary norms:** membership
vows, church constitutions, denominational
confessions (Augsburg, Westminster, Thirty-
Nine Articles) are all traditions guiding
interpretation.

The takeaway:

Everyone stands in **traditions**. Catholics distinguish between:

- Apostolic Tradition (the living transmission
of Christ's teaching through the Church,
safeguarded by the Magisterium).

- Human traditions (customs and practices
that can be helpful but are not binding).

So, when someone says, "We follow the Bible
alone," the fair question is: which traditions taught
you what the Bible is, and how to read it? That is
where the case for apostolic Tradition becomes not
just historical, but necessary.

Quick Reference Table

Objection and "Proof-text"	Catholic Counter-text	One-line Catholic Note
"Eucharist is symbolic." (Jn 6:63)	Jn 6:51–55; 1 Cor 11:27–29	Jesus insists His flesh is actual food; unworthy reception profanes the Body and Blood.
"Confess to God alone." (1 Jn 1:9; Ps 51)	Jn 20:21–23; Jas 5:16	Christ gave the Apostles authority to forgive sins; we confess and receive absolution
"Peter is not the rock; no papacy." (1 Cor 10:4; Mt 16:23)	Mt 16:18–19; Lk 22:31–32; Jn 21:15–17; Is 22:22	Jesus renames Peter "Rock," gives him the keys, prays that he strengthen the brethren, and commands him to shepherd.

"One mediator— so no saints/ Mary." (1 Tm 2:5)	1 Tm 2:1-4; Rv 5:8; Jn 2:1-11; Lk 1:48	Christ, the sole Mediator, welcomes intercession within His Body; the saints present prayers; "all generations" honor Mary.
"Images are idolatry." (Ex 20:4-5)	Ex 25:18-22; Nm 21:8-9	God forbids the worship of images, but He does not forbid the creation of sacred images that point to Him
"Faith alone— works do not matter." (Eph 2:8-9; Rom 3:28)	Jas 2:24; Gal 5:6; Phil 2:12-13	We are saved by grace through living faith that works through love.
"Tradition is condemned." (Mk 7:8; Col 2:8)	2 Thes 2:15; 1 Cor 11:2	Scripture condemns human traditions that nullify God's word, but commands apostolic Tradition (word and letter).

How We Got the Bible

Ask almost anyone, "Where did the Bible come from?" and the most common answer is, "God gave it to us." That is true—but how did He deliver it? As Henry Graham explains in *Where We Got the Bible*, God did not drop a bound volume from heaven. He gave us Christ, who founded a Church; from that Church's preaching and worship came the writings, and through that Church's discernment came the canon—the authoritative list of inspired books.

1) Church first, then Bible (apostolic age):

Jesus chose and taught the Apostles and sent them to preach. For years, the Gospel was handed on by word and sacrament. Traditionally, two of the twelve Apostles wrote Gospels: Matthew and John. The other two canonical Gospel writers—Mark and Luke—were not among the Twelve (Mark was a companion of Peter; Luke a companion of Paul). Others wrote letters to specific communities. These writings were read at worship alongside the Old Testament, copied, and shared. You can already see: Scripture arises within the Church's life, not outside it.

2) Many writings, one faith (second to fourth centuries):

By the second and third centuries, churches across the Roman world were using a core set of books we all recognize (the four Gospels, Acts, and most of the Pauline letters). At the same time, a few texts were disputed in some regions (e.g., Hebrews, James, Revelation). Additionally, other Christian writings circulated—the Didache, Shepherd of Hermas, and 1 Clement—were edifying but not universally recognized as inspired. Graham's simple point: Christians needed a trustworthy, standard list for reading in the liturgy and teaching the faithful.

3) Recognizing the canon (late fourth and fifth centuries):

The Church clarified the New Testament canon in the West through Rome (382) under Pope Damasus, and the regional councils of Hippo (393) and Carthage (397; reaffirmed 419)—all of which reflected the books long read in the churches. The Old Testament used by Christians included the books found in the Septuagint (the Greek Scriptures widely used by early Christians). Later, during the Reformation, some of these books (Tobit, Judith, Wisdom, Sirach, Baruch, 1-2 Maccabees, and the Greek parts of Esther/Daniel) were moved to an "Apocrypha" section or dropped by certain Protestants; the Catholic Church continued to receive them as deuterocanonical—part of the Bible from the beginning of Christian usage.

4) The Vulgate and preservation (Jerome to the monasteries):

At Rome's request, St. Jerome produced a reliable Latin translation—the Vulgate—which became the standard Bible of the West. For a thousand years, monks and cathedral clerics painstakingly copied, corrected, and preserved biblical manuscripts in scriptoria. Henry Graham emphasizes this simple debt: without the Church's custody, much of Scripture would have been lost to war, weather, and time.

5) Practice proves structure (worship shaped the canon):

Christians did not keep Scripture as a private reference manual. They proclaimed it at Mass, preached it, sang it, and prayed it. The Bible was lived within a visible community under the leadership of pastors (bishops, presbyters, deacons). That is why, in Graham's telling, it makes no sense to set "Bible against Church." The Bible came through the Church and is safest within the Church that recognized it.

6) Printing press and controversy (fifteenth and sixteenth centuries):

The printing press multiplied Bibles—and opinions. Disputes over which books belong and what they mean intensified. In 1546, the Council of Trent solemnly defined the long-received canon to end confusion: not creating a new Bible but ending a debate about the old one.

7) What this means for you:

- Saying "God gave us the Bible" is right; saying "the Bible chose itself" is not. God used His Church to recognize and safeguard the inspired books.

- The Bible does not include a table of contents; the Church recognized it.

- The same Christ who gave us Scripture also gave us a Church—"*the pillar and foundation of the truth*" (1 Tm 3:15)—to preserve and interpret it authentically.

One-minute takeaway (Graham's heartbeat in brief):

We owe the Bible, in human terms, to the Catholic Church—it is its preaching that produced the writings, its worship that preserved them, its councils that recognized the canon, its monks who copied it, and its teaching office that guards it. God gave us the Bible through the Church He founded.

An Invitation Before We Pray

Despite disagreements and the wounds of history, the Catholic Church does not answer with hostility; she opens her arms to her separated brothers and sisters. Many have already come home. I know the refrain—*"That church didn't do anything for me; I didn't get anything out of it."* Catholics say this, too. But Christ's Church is not designed to coddle feelings; she is ordered to **holiness**. Our Lord did not say, "Follow your feelings," but, "If any man will come after me, let him deny himself, and take up his cross, and follow me" (Mt 16:24).

Belief alone is not enough; even the devil believes in Christ (Jas 2:10), but he insists on his own way; he wants to take his own path. Becoming a disciple of Christ may not always feel good; in fact, it will hurt like hell at times and turn your life inside out, but it is the path we must take if we truly want to follow Christ.

Worship is first about what we give to God—faith, adoration, obedience—not merely what we "get." And grace is not a tarp thrown over a wreck; it is power to be made new: a new heart (Ezek 36:26), a new creation (2 Cor 5:17), a mind **renewed** (Rom 12:2), trained by grace to live godly (Tit 2:11-12). We "work out" our salvation precisely because God works in us (Phil 2:12-13). This is the Church's mission: to cooperate with that grace through Scripture, sacrament, and discipline, so that Christ does not merely **cover** our sin but **conforms** us to Himself.

And so, rather than argue to the last proof-text, I want to close this appeal in the only fitting way—by asking the Lord who prayed "that they all may be one" (Jn 17:21) to finish the work He began. If any of this has stirred something in you, bring it with you into the prayer that follows. Bring your questions. Bring your Bible. Bring your desire for holiness that goes beyond a feeling. The Church's arms are open—not to win an argument, but to welcome you home to the fullness Christ intended.

A Prayer to Protestants

Dear brothers and sisters in Christ,

I wrote this book to show not only the theology of the Church Jesus founded, but also the simple logic behind it. For over five centuries since the Reformation, sincere attempts to "reform" have too often resulted in fragmentation—new pulpits, new statements of faith, new interpretations—each begun in goodwill yet multiplying differences. If you have ever felt the strain of that, you are not alone.

Some of us left the Church young, more out of restlessness than reasoning. Later, an evangelical friend reintroduced us to Jesus in a way that felt warm, urgent, and personal. Often, that invitation came with the refrain, *"Catholics are wrong."* If that was your path, I understand why it resonated. As children, we didn't yet grasp **what** the Church was or **why** she claimed to teach with authority. A simpler message—*"just believe"*—sounded like freedom.

Others were never exposed to the Catholic Church beyond caricatures. You were told that Catholics "add to the Gospel," or "worship Mary," or "replace Scripture with tradition." You heard confident voices, each with a verse or two, each certain the others were mistaken. Much of it was said in good faith. I heard those same voices. However, looking back, I often heard a less-than Gospel: *you don't need Confession—go straight to God; you don't need the saints—God can't possibly use their intercession; you don't need any visible Church—just the Bible and your heart.*

Yet the God who speaks also builds; the Christ who **saves** also **gathers**; the Spirit who inspires Scripture also guards its meaning in a living Body.

A real relationship is never only a label; it's a communion—sometimes comforting, sometimes demanding, always purifying. The Church, Christ's Bride, is that communion. She calls us to repentance and to the sacraments, to love Scripture **in** the worship that birthed it, and to a unity that is more than sentiment. Unity costs. It asks us to let Jesus be Lord not only of our hearts, but of our judgments—especially when our judgments feel sufficient.

So here is my prayer—for you, for me, for all who love the Lord Jesus:

Lord Jesus Christ,

You prayed, *"that they all may be one… that the world may believe"* (Jn 17:21). Heal the wounds of our divisions. Where pride has hardened us, give humility; where fear has closed us, give courage; where hurt has lingered, give mercy. Teach us to read Your Word with the Church that received it, to recognize Your voice **in** the flock You gathered, and to trust the Spirit You promised would guide that flock "into all truth."

Father,

You built a household, not a crowd. When we are tempted to live as isolated interpreters, remind us that You gave Apostles and pastors and teachers "for the edifying of the body of Christ… that we be no more children, tossed to and fro" (Eph 4:11–14). Make us eager to test our convictions against the whole of Your revelation: Scripture proclaimed, sacraments celebrated, doctrine preserved, saints raised up.

Holy Spirit,

Grant us docility. If we have accepted less than the fullness of Your gifts, draw us onward. If we have spoken carelessly about one another, teach our lips charity and our minds patience. Give us the courage to ask the hard questions—*How did we get the Bible? Who judges when readings collide? Where is the Church Christ promised would not fail?* —and the honesty to follow the answers wherever You lead.

For my Protestant friends who love Jesus: thank you for your zeal, your love of Scripture, your boldness in witness. Please hear this invitation not as a victory lap, but as a homeward call. Come and see the **continuity**: the same Creed, the same Eucharist, the same apostolic laying on of hands, across languages and centuries. Bring your questions.

Bring your Bible. Come to Mass, read one Father (Ignatius, Irenaeus), study the councils that guarded the truth you already cherish. If the Catholic Church is merely human, she will not endure. If she is what Christ says—"*the church of the living God, the pillar and ground of the truth*" (1 Tim 3:15)—then you will find not a rival to Jesus, but the **Bride** who bears His voice.

Lord, make us one—not by lowering the bar of truth, but by raising our hearts to it. Give us the grace to prefer Your wisdom to our own and to remain in the **boat** You built, even when seas are rough. And grant that, in our lifetime, we may taste more fully the unity You prayed for, to the glory of the Father, with You and the Holy Ghost, one God, world without end. Amen.

BIBLIOGRAPHY

Scripture

- The Holy Bible: King James Version. Hendrickson, 2009.

Magisterial / Conciliar Documents & Reference Collections

- *Catechism of the Catholic Church*. 2nd ed. Libreria Editrice Vaticana, 1997.

- Denzinger, Heinrich, and Peter Hünermann, eds. *Enchiridion Symbolorum: A Compendium of Creeds, Definitions, and Declarations on Matters of Faith and Morals*. 43rd ed. Ignatius Press, 2012.

- Joint International Commission for Theological Dialogue between the Roman Catholic Church and the Orthodox Church. *Synodality and Primacy during the First Millennium: Towards a Common Understanding in Service to the Unity of the Church*. Chieti, September 21, 2016. Accessed January 9, 2026. *https://www.christianunity.va/content/unitacristiani/en/dialoghi/sezione-orientale/chiese-ortodosse-di-tradizione-bizantina/commissione-mista-internazionale-per-il-dialogo-teologico-tra-la/documenti-di-dialogo/testo-in-inglese1.html*.

- Schroeder, H. J., trans. *The Canons and Decrees of the Council of Trent*. TAN Books, 1978.

- Tanner, Norman P., ed. *Decrees of the Ecumenical Councils*. 2 vols. Georgetown University Press, 1990.

- Vatican Council I. *Pastor Aeternus (On the Infallible Teaching Authority of the Roman Pontiff)*. 1870.

- Vatican Council II. *Dei Verbum (Dogmatic Constitution on Divine Revelation)*. 1965.

Church Fathers / Early Sources (Primary)

- *The Apostolic Fathers*. Translated by Michael W. Holmes. 3rd ed. Baker Academic, 2007. (*Includes the Didache and letters of Ignatius, etc.*)

- Cyprian of Carthage. "On the Unity of the Catholic Church." In *The Lapsed and the Unity of the Catholic Church*, translated by Maurice Bévenot. Newman Press, 1957.

- Eusebius of Caesarea. *Ecclesiastical History*. Translated by Paul L. Maier. Kregel, 2007.

- Irenaeus of Lyons. *Against Heresies*. Translated by Dominic J. Unger and John J. Dillon. Paulist Press, 1992.

- Justin Martyr. *The First and Second Apologies*. Translated by Leslie William Barnard. Paulist Press, 1997.

- Athanasius. *On the Incarnation*. Translated by John Behr. St. Vladimir's Seminary Press, 2011.

Canon of Scripture / "How We Got the Bible"

- Bruce, F. F. *The Canon of Scripture*. InterVarsity Press, 1988.

- Graham, Henry G. *Where We Got the Bible: Our Debt to the Catholic Church*. TAN Books, 1997.

- Metzger, Bruce M. *The Canon of the New Testament: Its Origin, Development, and Significance*. Clarendon Press, 1987.

- Michuta, Gary. *Why Catholic Bibles Are Bigger*. Revised 2nd ed. Catholic Answers Press, 2017.

Development of Doctrine / Authority / Tradition

- Newman, John Henry. *An Essay on the Development of Christian Doctrine*. University of Notre Dame Press, 1989.

- Ott, Ludwig. *Fundamentals of Catholic Dogma*. 4th ed. TAN Books, 1974.

- Ratzinger, Joseph (Benedict XVI). *Called to Communion: Understanding the Church Today*. Ignatius Press, 1996.

- Sullivan, Francis A. *From Apostles to Bishops: The Development of the Episcopacy in the Early Church*. Paulist Press, 2001.

- Dulles, Avery. *A History of Apologetics*. Ignatius Press, 2005.

Papal Primacy / Petrine Office

- Cullmann, Oscar. *Peter: Disciple, Apostle, Martyr*. Westminster, 1953.

- Ray, Stephen K. *Upon This Rock: St. Peter and the Primacy of Rome in Scripture and the Early Church*. Ignatius Press, 1999.

- Schatz, Klaus. *Papal Primacy: From Its Origins to the Present*. Liturgical Press, 1996.

The Trinity / Nicaea and Arianism

- Ayres, Lewis. *Nicaea and Its Legacy: An Approach to Fourth-Century Trinitarian Theology*. Oxford University Press, 2004.

- Kelly, J. N. D. *Early Christian Doctrines*. Rev. ed. A & C Black, 1978.

Eucharist / Liturgy / Early Worship

- Jungmann, Josef A. *The Mass of the Roman Rite: Its Origins and Development*. 2 vols. Christian Classics, 1986.

- Pitre, Brant. *Jesus and the Jewish Roots of the Eucharist: Unlocking the Secrets of the Last Supper*. Image, 2016.

- Ratzinger, Joseph (Benedict XVI). *The Spirit of the Liturgy*. Ignatius Press, 2000.

Protestantism, Fragmentation, and Sola Scriptura (Dialogue Partners)

- Charlie Kirk. *"Is the Pope Legit? Catholicism v. Protestantism Debate Ft. Michael Knowles."* YouTube video, accessed December 30, 2025. *https://www.youtube.com/watch?v=6Z-bBll-1tg*

- Mathison, Keith A. *The Shape of Sola Scriptura*. Canon Press, 2001.

- McGrath, Alister. *Christianity's Dangerous Idea: The Protestant Revolution—A History from the Sixteenth Century to the Twenty-First*. HarperOne, 2007.

Marian Doctrine (Historical Notes, Luther, etc.)

- Oberman, Heiko A. *Luther: Man Between God and the Devil*. Yale University Press, 1989.

- Pelikan, Jaroslav. *Mary Through the Centuries: Her Place in the History of Culture*. Yale University Press, 1996.

"Motives of Credibility"

- Dulles, Avery. *The Assurance of Things Hoped For: A Theology of Christian Faith*. Oxford University Press, 1994.

- Feingold, Lawrence. *Motives of Credibility for Faith*. Association of Hebrew Catholics Lecture Series, "Introduction to Theology: Faith Seeking Understanding," Series 12, Talk #7 (PDF). Association of Hebrew Catholics, Fall 2013.

- Kreeft, Peter. *Fundamentals of the Faith: Essays in Christian Apologetics*. Ignatius Press, 1988.

Additional Resources

Bible Verses

Unity & Oneness

- John 17:21, 23
- Romans 15:5-6
- 1 Corinthians 1:10
- Ephesians 4:3-6
- Philippians 2:2
- Colossians 3:14-15
- 1 Corinthians 12:12-13

Christ Establishes & Governs His Church (Peter, the Keys)

- Isaiah 22:22
- Matthew 16:18-19
- Luke 22:32
- John 21:15-17

Apostolic Authority & Mission

- Luke 10:16
- John 15:16
- John 16:12-15
- John 20:21-23; 20:22
- Matthew 28:16-20
- Acts 1:8

Apostolic Succession & Ordination

- Acts 6:6
- Acts 13:2-3
- Acts 14:23
- Titus 1:5
- 1 Timothy 4:14
- 1 Timothy 5:22
- 2 Timothy 2:2

Ecclesial Authority & Discipline (Binding/ Loosing; "Tell it to the Church")

- Matthew 18:15-17
- Matthew 18:18

Scripture, Tradition, & Interpretation

- 2 Thessalonians 2:15
- 2 Thessalonians 3:6

- 1 Corinthians 11:2
- John 21:25
- Acts 8:30–31
- 2 Peter 3:16

Church as Pillar & Magisterium / Obedience to Leaders

- 1 Timothy 3:15
- Ephesians 2:19–22
- Ephesians 4:11–16
- Hebrews 13:17

Guarding Sound Doctrine & the Deposit of Faith

- 2 Timothy 4:3
- Galatians 1:8
- Jude 1:3
- 1 John 4:1

Trust, Obedience, & Christian Charity (Discipleship in Practice)

- Proverbs 3:5
- Proverbs 16:3
- James 1:22
- 2 Timothy 2:24–25
- 1 Peter 4:8

Visibility & Reality of the Church

- Acts 8:3 (persecution of the Church as a visible body)

This is only a brief starter list of commonly cited passages for unity, authority, and apostolic continuity. For more Scripture references organized by topic, see the **Catholic Bible Verse Finder** at _CatholicApologetics.com_. And always read these verses in context, within the living faith of the Church that safeguards their authentic meaning.

Recommended Reading

1. Aquilina, Mike, *The Fathers of the Church*

2. Aquilina, Mike, *The Mass of the Early Christians*

3. Augustine, St., *Confessions*

4. *Catechism of the Catholic Church*

5. D'Ambrosio, Marcellino, *Who Were the Church Fathers? From Clement of Rome to Gregory the Great*

6. D'Ambrosio, Marcellino, and Andrew Swafford, *What We Believe*

7. de Sales, St. Francis, *The Catholic Controversy*

8. Gasser, Bishop Vincent, *The Gift of Infallibility*

9. Graham, Henry, *Where We Got the Bible*

10. Hahn, Scott, *Rome Sweet Home*

11. Keating, Karl, *Catholicism and Fundamentalism: The Attack on "Romanism" by "Bible Christians"*

12. Kreeft, Peter, and Ronald Tacelli, *Handbook of Christian Apologetics: Hundreds of Answers to Crucial Questions*

13. Merton, Thomas, *The Seven Storey Mountain*

14. Pitre, Brant, *Jesus and the Jewish Roots of the Eucharist*

15. Sheed, Frank, *Theology and Sanity*

16. Staples, Tim, *Catholic Answers to Common Objections*

YouTube

These are just a few of the many YouTube channels available. If you are new, I would recommend starting with the first three:

Shameless Popery: detailed response videos to criticisms of the Catholic objections.

How to Be Christian: how Protestants twist and read the Bible.

Word on Fire / Bishop Robert Barron: high-quality teaching on doctrine, culture, and evangelization; short videos and podcast clips.

EWTN, Journey Home: detailed conversion stories.

Catholic Answers: live Q&A, debates, bite-sized apologetics; huge archive. A great first stop.

The Counsel of Trent (Trent Horn): calm, evidence-driven takedowns of common objections; interviews and debates.

Pints with Aquinas (Matt Fradd): Long-form conversations with scholars, apologists, and clergy; Catholic philosophy/theology with an accessible tone.

Ascension Presents (Fr. Mike Schmitz and team): short, pastoral videos answering practical and theological questions; highly shareable.

Reason and Theology (Michael Lofton): interviews, roundtables, and critiques on theology/history with an apologetics edge.

Patristic Pillars (William Albrecht): early Church Fathers, Marian doctrine, debates with Protestants/Orthodox (patristics-heavy).

Scholastic Answers (Christian Wagner): detailed academic tone, intermediate academic style.

Web

WhyCatholic.com: resources and easy-to-read articles

Catholic Answers / _https://Catholic.com:_ books, videos, and answers

Jesse Romero / _https://jesseromero.com_**:** straight talk, easy to understand

Magis Center / _https://magiscenter.com_**:** faith, science, and reason

EWTN / _ewtn.com_**:** apologetics, education

Crossroads Initiative / _https://crossroadsinitiative.com_**:** Dr. Marcellino D'Ambrosio—podcasts, videos, writings

San Juan Catholic Seminars / _https://catholicapologetics.com_**:** Beginning Apologetics Series, and Catholic Verse Finder